Basic Topics in Mathematics for Dyslexics

Basic Topics in Mathematics for Dyslexics

by

ANNE HENDERSON and **ELAINE MILES**

Consultants, Dyslexia Unit, University of Wales, Bangor

Consultant in Dyslexia
PROFESSOR MARGARET SNOWLING
University of York

W
WHURR PUBLISHERS
LONDON AND PHILADELPHIA

© 2001 Whurr Publishers
First published 2001 by
Whurr Publishers Ltd
19b Compton Terrace, London N1 2UN, England and
325 Chestnut Street, Philadelphia PA 19106, USA

Reprinted 2002 and 2004

British Library Cataloguing in Publication Data
A catalogue record for this book is available from the
British Library.

ISBN: 1 86156 211 X

Printed and bound in the UK by Athenaeum Press Ltd,
Gateshead, Tyne & Wear

Contents

Chapter 19   **127**

A useful procedure for tackling mathematics problems

Preface

It is now clear that dyslexics may have specific difficulties in particular aspects of mathematics, yet have considerable potential in other areas (Steeves, 1983; Miles and Miles, 1992; Chinn and Ashcroft, 1993). There are some distinguished physicists and mathematicians who nevertheless have found difficulty with basic mechanical learning tasks such as multiplication tables. Mathematics involves a great range of abilities – the more spatial ones, e.g. geometry, are not usually a problem for dyslexics. It is the number areas of mathematics, together with difficulties of organization of their work, that often prevent dyslexics from using their mathematical potential to the full.

The original motivation behind this book was to encourage specialist dyslexia teachers to help dyslexic children with these particular problems in mathematics. When the need for this was first realized at Bangor, we knew that our experienced team of teachers at the Dyslexia Unit would readily understand from their work in the literacy field the *sort* of errors to expect in mathematics, but the teachers themselves felt very unsure of their own competence in the subject itself. Whatever level they had reached in mathematics at school, they had done what they had been told without really understanding what it was all about, and therefore did not feel in a position to give others the real understanding that would be necessary.

It therefore occurred to Elaine Miles that we might pick out a number of topics that would be particularly valuable to teach to a dyslexic pupil and explain very clearly in 'teachers' notes' the gist of what a teacher needed to get over, while separating these topics as much as possible so that it would be possible to teach them singly without any danger of being led into other areas where the teacher might feel insecure; we could then add suggestions how to teach them and materials that they might use. Then perhaps even the most maths-phobic teacher might feel encouraged to pick a topic and 'have a go'. Even to teach a few basic topics would help a child, as it is often quite basic matters that have not been grasped. A small booklet on these lines was produced within the Dyslexia Unit at Bangor. When Anne Henderson joined in this endeavour, her vast experience in teaching mathematics to dyslexics, especially as head of the special maths unit at St. David's College, Llandudno, made possible a much bigger enterprise for a wider readership.

We were encouraged by reviews of the earlier Bangor book, *Dyslexia and Mathematics*, to which we both contributed, to think that some of what we had to offer would be useful to other pupils besides dyslexics. We have therefore included some advice at the beginning on the difficulties that a teacher may expect dyslexics to have in mathematics, together with a checklist; we discuss assessment and indicate what kind of approaches are helpful, in the hope that ordinary class teachers would also use the book with pupils who would benefit from it. Nevertheless we have not attempted to cover the whole curriculum even at this basic level, only areas where dyslexics particularly need help.

Of course, making the topics completely separable has not been wholly possible – some topics cannot be taught until others are secure, so we have had to put them in some sort of order – but in these cases we have tried to say so. There is certainly no need to go straight through the book chapter by chapter. Teachers can select what they want to teach.

In the Appendix are some notes on the new 'National Numeracy Strategy'. It is important that teachers read this to realize what valuable contributions are introduced by this Strategy, which will be being used in schools in future. The flexibility and variety of methods will be helpful to dyslexics, although the pace set is likely to be too great. Among other recommendations it stresses the importance of multisensory teaching, and of teaching the language used in mathematics, which we have always advocated. We have been influenced by the Strategy to allow for horizontal working as well as vertical, and to make a greater use of number lines. In the case of dyslexics, however, we think it important that they also learn how our notation system works on a ten basis, by using multisensory blocks, trading, etc., and saying what they are doing as they do it – as we have described in this book. It is not difficult if approached in that way, and dyslexics otherwise tend to have difficulty with place value.

Also in the Appendix are various visual aids and exercises relevant to different sections, and a list of useful materials, books and computer software. Answers to the sheets of practice sums at the end of sections are also there. (Where questions were included at intervals inside a section, the answers are at the end of that section.)

We hope we may be forgiven for using the pronoun 'he' throughout, as a very large proportion of our dyslexic pupils are male, and it is tedious to keep saying 'he or she'.

Anne Henderson
Elaine Miles
Bangor, May 2000.

References

Chinn SJ and Ashcroft JR (1993) Mathematics for Dyslexics: a Teaching Handbook. London: Whurr.

Miles TR and Miles E (eds) (1992) Dyslexia and Mathematics . London: Routledge.

Steeves KJ (1983) Memory as a factor in the computational efficiency of dyslexic children with high abstract reasoning ability. Annals of Dyslexia 33, 141–52.

Note

In the Appendices there are some worksheets (A2–A10, pp. 132–151), which may be photocopied for classroom use only.

Chapter 1
General advice on teaching

How to help

Dyslexic pupils do not learn if they are just told about a mathematics topic orally; they have to be taught through multi-sensory methods if the teaching is to have any impact on their acquisition of mathematical skills. They need to use practical apparatus to find out for themselves, but also need to talk about what they are discovering. Frequently the important concept within a topic has to be pointed out to them, as they will not see it clearly through over-anxiety.

Sometimes they will need to say aloud what they have found out, or maybe they will need to draw it. Often they like to use colour to illustrate their findings and this seems to make certain facts stick in their memory. Other pupils need to have what they say recorded on to an audio tape so that they can replay it to understand properly what they have discovered. Some like to use big motor movements (like walking big steps to measure). We should also take into consideration whether a pupil learns best with two dimensions through pictures and diagrams, or would prefer three-dimensional apparatus.

The approach throughout should be one that promotes confidence by being structured, systematic, building on strengths, linking to previous knowledge, and dividing the topic into easy steps that the pupil understands. An atmosphere that puts pupils at their ease will be most conducive to learning. If a teacher sees a method being used that is unusual, is very long, but works, it is better to allow the pupil to continue that method until he himself decides that a change is needed; telling him that his method is wrong will create fear and insecurity, and may lead him to give up on mathematics altogether.

1

Language

New language and symbols should be introduced carefully and discussed. Teachers should also be aware that readability schemes are inappropriate in the case of books on mathematics, and teachers themselves will have to look critically at text in maths books and assess its suitability.

Multisensory materials

Teachers who are used to teaching literacy skills to dyslexics will know that large and small motor movements, tracing, using an audio tape recorder, computers, pictures, diagrams, 2D and 3D materials all help in reinforcement of the topic being taught.

Pupils should be encouraged to build up a special maths book, in which they record – using colour, pasted pictures, rhymes, mnemonics etc. – under topic headings, any important methods and notes that they want for reference later.

Blank index cards are also useful; the topic and method are written in easy language on one side and an example on the other and they can be kept handy in a small box. With older pupils the notes are best put on to larger index cards and kept in alphabetical order in an index box. At examination times these cards can be put on to walls so that they make a visual impact.

Obviously if a pupil is used to recording with mind maps he should be encouraged to do the same with his maths notes as that way he will feel more secure and sure that his own ways are of value.

Learning styles

Teachers should try to observe and discover by discussion the preferred learning styles of their pupils to see if they are:

- simultaneous, intuitive learners – these are pupils who will give an answer very quickly, which may be wrong but is often correct, but who will have no idea how they found the answer. They are holistic in their approach, viewing a question overall and then making a judgement.
- sequential, logical learners – these are pupils who seem to get bogged down in the details, and at times are unable to see where to get an answer from. They like to go through a series of set steps, but have not quite the sequential skills necessary.
- learners who prefer to listen, think, draw, touch or see in order to learn and understand. Although a multisensory approach is mandatory for all teaching of dyslexics, we need to know which approach will best 'kick-start' the learning process.

Types of assessment

A good way of spotting errors is to observe a student working, especially if the teacher is in a position to ask him gently to explain his method. However it is not always possible for a busy teacher to find time to do this.

SATS tests now provide a good record of a student's work. After looking through the test and noting the types of errors, perhaps the teacher can find time to sit with the student and ask him to talk about his methods.

It is important that he is allowed time to explain just what he has done and why before his method is condemned by a teacher who is not accustomed to the variety of strategies and methods that dyslexic students may use. If possible, an audio tape recording should be made of the student's explanation of a particular method and at the end his answers played back to him. Often he will self-correct, realizing that what he has said is not what he meant. Humour in such situations helps to lighten the atmosphere.

More informally and light-heartedly, a teacher can gain some insight on his addition and subtraction methods by setting some magic squares (see Appendix). These involve doing addition and subtraction in order to make each line, horizontal, vertical and diagonal, add up to the same amount. Start, of course, with the small number puzzles, and notice whether he attempts to do them in his head and to what level he attempts this.

- Does he attempt mental arithmetic beyond his powers? (He probably needs practice in addition facts.)
- When he writes the sums down – possibly at your suggestion – note his procedures, errors, where he puts carrying figures and whether he seems to understand the function of these.
- Try to use maths books with squares of 0.7 cms.
- Maths books for some reason do not have margins, so help your student with practice in using his ruler to draw them in. Students who are dyspraxic, or who cannot handle a ruler and a pencil simultaneously, will need appropriate help.
- Always try to observe your student's writing of numbers, since faults in this, e.g. a 5 looking like a 3, may be the cause of errors.
- Observe also his habits when working on paper. Does he stray from the columns, fail to observe margins, set out his sums in a disorderly way on the page, fail to use a ruler for straight lines?
- Try to help him keep a tidy page by adopting a positive attitude, always encouraging, so that he will know that he is progressing towards high standards in his work.

Published tests

In assessment we are trying to find out at what point to begin to help a pupil. If a pupil completes a published test we should, as well as marking it, be looking to see if he is struggling with particular difficulties in mathematics that are typical of dyslexics.

Teachers should also be looking to see how quickly he reads, as well as noting whether it is a struggle both to read and to understand the words. Problems with both speed and understanding will limit his performance, especially in a timed test.

Particular difficulties of dyslexics as they affect mathematics

Short-term memory weaknesses affect them in various ways, in recording sequences accurately and memorizing (days of the week, months, multiplication tables especially because they have to keep two processes going at once, the sequence of numbers that they are multiplying and the answers). Mental calculations are also difficult and carrying through an algorithm consistently, remembering which direction to work a sum (left–right or right–left). They may also make mistakes in calculator procedures.

Language-learning weaknesses make it difficult for them to learn all the different codes used in mathematics – the meaning of all the symbols, place value, how fractions and decimals must be treated differently from whole numbers, the ways of recording money and time. There are other language difficulties too:

- the contrast between precise mathematical terms e.g. 'dimensions' 'square' as opposed to vague popular ones e.g. 'size' and 'square' as in Trafalgar Square (which is not square at all)
- as well as the actual reading-level of the text of a question (which may be high), the different approach needed for reading a mathematical problem text as opposed to a story text. In the former, colourful details are largely irrelevant; what needs to be picked out are the given data and the relations between them. Pupils also need practice in turning the ordinary language used in a maths question into the necessary sum.

  See the diagrams showing the variety of everyday expressions used to express addition, subtraction etc. at the end of the relevant sections, and also the chapter on tackling maths problems, (pp. 131–3.)

Read also:
> Miles, E. (1992) Chapter 4 – 'Reading and writing in mathematics' in T.R.Miles and E.Miles (eds) *Dyslexia and Mathematics* London: Routledge

Organizational weaknesses affect their grasp of timetables and their ability to set out work clearly and systematically. If they are also poorly co-ordinated their written work may be difficult to read, numbers not clear, etc.

Below you will find a checklist of items that you may like to use to record the various points where your pupil needs your help.

Dyslexic pupils may have difficulty with all or some of the following topics:

- days of the week in order
- months of the year in order
- times tables
- specific difficulties with the passage of time and solving time-related problems
- reading numbers accurately
- telling the time
- simple computation
  - addition
  - subtraction
  - multiplication
  - division
- connecting the correct name to the number, e.g. 4 read as five
- counting forwards and backwards
- connecting the correct name to the mathematical symbol and then remembering just what process that symbol represents
- doing mental calculations
- using money correctly
- have trouble with left/right, forward/backward, before/after, above/below
- noticing that a mathematical symbol has changed i.e. + to −
- transferring from one topic to another
- keeping columns straight, e.g. tens under tens column
- spatial difficulties causing confusion because of the untidy presentation
- dyspraxic problems making the numbers difficult to read

- language difficulties having an influence on any reading and writing connected to mathematics
- putting the correct number into a calculator
- pressing the correct symbol key on a calculator
- decimal point i.e. difficulty with place value
- great difficulty or phobia with fractions
- remembering the wrong pattern in a method.

Chapter 2
Estimation

The importance of estimation

The importance of developing estimation skills in mathematics from an early age cannot be emphasized enough. Estimation is not to be scorned as just 'guessing'; it is a skill in predicting beforehand the order of magnitude of an answer at which one is aiming, thus focusing expectations correctly, and making it easy to spot and correct slips that may end in distorting the answer grossly.

Estimation is a skill that all students need to acquire in order to perform simple arithmetical tasks in ordinary life. They need to acquire it early in school life in order to become confident and proficient as they grow older. Once the procedure is understood and accepted as the norm before working out a sum, a pattern has been established which forms the basis of good practice in mathematics. Teachers need to be aware of the importance of this practice and incorporate it in all their lessons.

Estimations involving multiplication or division are obviously more difficult and require much patience to teach, as dyslexics do not know their tables and guess the answers to these rather wildly.

Proficiency in estimation and approximation can boost a student's confidence in his mathematical ability. Not only does it mean that he is able to make a sensible guess at the size of an answer, but also that he is able to use a strategy to back it up. The fact that he is able to find some sort of answer probably means that he has understood the question and has already decided on a procedure that will allow him to reach the solution, and this is helpful for the teacher.

Estimation skills help a student to acquire correct and capable use of a calculator; he will be able to self-correct if his answer is very different from the one expected. Finally, estimation skills are very important in life outside school. It will provide him with a survival kit after his school days are over.

For instance, in dealing with money:

We need to be able to estimate roughly how much money is involved in the following:

to buy:
- a loaf of bread
- a bottle/carton of milk
- a newspaper

to pay for:
- my bus fare into town

to see if I can afford:
- several items of food at the supermarket
- to take more than one person to the theatre/cinema
- a taxi ride home
- a particular article of clothing
- a round of drinks

to check:
- that the change I receive is correct
- whether an estimate given by a workman is reasonable
- that the percentage discount is correct on a holiday or on an expensive purchase like a car
- that the regular payments to be paid for hire purchase are correct – and to be aware that arithmetical skills may be not quite adequate at this level, and seek help.

Difficulties with estimation

Pupils generally are not keen to estimate, but dyslexic pupils are even less enthusiastic to take on the extra task of trying to give a rough or even an educated guess at the size of an answer. As teachers, we should encourage a pupil to give an answer, using easy numbers instead of the exact ones, e.g. 10 instead of 8 or 13. However, many pupils say that they do not want to do this. Rounding up or down seems to cause them real mental anguish; they struggle so much with the exact numbers, that to use similar ones and then have to repeat the process with the exact ones is altogether too demanding.

Consequently estimation needs to be done in easy stages so that they become confident with regard to this important aspect of mathematics. In every topic the estimation stages need to be understood and practised by the pupil until he has gained expertise and can move on to the next stage.

Stage 1 – Easy numbers

In a quiet informal way, when a pupil is beginning to acquire mathematical skills, talk to him and ask him to give a guess as to the size of the answer. Discuss what 'easy numbers' are, and how by thinking through procedures he may find a way to tackle the problem.

Easy numbers are those which the student understands the value of and can manipulate easily. If a teacher explains a topic in the first place using easy numbers, students will begin to accept that they make the topic easily comprehensible. Some obvious 'easy numbers' are 2, 5 and 10, as a student meets them early in life and they pose no threat. Obviously it is not always possible to use those particular numbers, but students will soon learn to find others close to the ones in the problem if they get accustomed to using this approach when they are young.

After easy numbers have been used to estimate, and then the exact answers obtained, move him gently forward to Stage 2.

Stage 2 – Rounding up or down to the nearest 10.

This is a skill that needs to be carefully taught. Dyslexic pupils may have problems with the word 'nearest'. They tend to think it is something to do with the *size* of the number. Working with a number line may help. It is best to start with a small range of 10s.

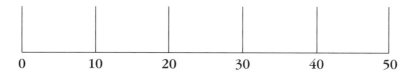

- Is 7 nearer to 10 or to 0?
- Is 12 nearer to 10 or to 20?
- Is 16 nearer to 10 or to 20?
- Is 41 nearer to 40 or to 50?

Also, they often reject e.g. that 30 is the nearest ten to 26, because 20 is nearest in form, being also in the 'twenties'. It is essential to spend some time on getting this clear, before moving on. Often by this stage they will be ready for more formal estimation work, which entails dividing a page in half, one half for the estimated answer, and the other half for the exact answer. In this way the pupil can see how accurate his estimates were. All four 'rules' need to be practised when numbers have been rounded so that different estimate strategies may be developed which the pupil can fully trust.

Rounding off a number when an approximate answer is required, e.g. 'to the nearer 10', involves taking it to the nearest 10. **When the number ends in 5, it must always be rounded off to the higher 10.**

e.g.   If we round off 5 the answer is 10
       If we round off 15 the answer is 20
       If we round off 35 the answer is 40
       If we round off 95 the answer is 100.

Stage 3 – Making an educated guess

This involves combining skills from stages 1 and 2, considering the question very carefully to get the best approximate size of the answer required, as in the following examples:

*   the price of 3 tins of paint, each costing £8.78
    Easy Numbers   £8.00 x 3 = £24.00
    Rounding   £9.00 x 3 = £27.00
    Educated Guess   It is somewhere between £24.00 and £27.00, but
                          nearer to £27.00, because £8.78 is nearer to
                          £9.00 than £8.00., so say £26.00

The exact answer is £26.34.

*   the cost of 4 cups of coffee @ 84p, and 3 scones @ 58p
    Easy Numbers   80 x 4   = 320p (8 x 4 and add 0 to the answer)
                          50 x 3   = 150p (5 x 3 and add 0 to the answer)
                          Total   = 470p
    Rounding   £1.00 x 4 = £4.00
                          60p x 3   = £1.80
                          Total   = £5.80
    Educated Guess   It is somewhere between £4.70 and £5.80, say £5.00

The exact answer is £5.10.

Stage 4 – Ignoring decimals

We use this skill when dealing with money, as in the above examples, but also when dealing with more precise measurements involving length, weight or capacity. If we need to know the combined length of two pieces of wood that are 3.68 cms. and 7.23 cms. the student could happily take 3+7 cms to get an approximate answer. Often when decimal numbers are combined with other units, students who have problems with the language of decimals become so anxious about recognising the unit that they forget their estimation skills. Therefore much practice is needed with different units until the student is quite sure that he can apply his estimation skills correctly.

Stage 5 – Using appropriate-sized numbers for specific cases

If amounts are very small or very large, e.g. weights of small items in grams on the one hand and cost of houses or populations of countries on the other, students have to be aware that the size of the estimated answer must accord with the actual question. This is important even in the early stages, but it is only when a student has developed good estimation skills that he will have to tackle questions with great detail or very large numbers. Therefore he has to be shown that the basic skills that he has developed in the earlier stages of estimation are still valid for more complex questions.

Chapter 3
Understanding number

Students like to see and recognize numbers in the shape of patterns and connect these up with digits. The connection is clearly made in the following diagram.

Word	Pattern	Digit
One	*	1
Two	* *	2
Three	* * *	3
Four	* * * *	4
Five	* * * * *	5
Six	* * * * * *	6
Seven	* * * * * * *	7
Eight	* * * * * * * *	8
Nine	* * * * * * * * *	9
Ten	* * * * * * * * * *	10

Figure 1.

The number line

A number line from 0 to 10 should be drawn with ten equal spaces being marked with lines as shown in Figure 2. When students are familiar with the number word – number pattern – number symbol (numeral) connection then it is possible to move on to using a number line to begin connecting the value of each individual number and its number pattern by its place on the number line.

Spelling number words

Dyslexic students do not always know how to spell the numbers 1 to 10. These could be written down the left-hand side of a card such as in Figure 1, p. 13, which can be folded into three sections vertically. The linking number patterns go in the middle section and the digit on the right. If the student visualizes certain colours and particular patterns for individual numbers, these should be recorded. This seems to be particularly important for the number 5. Later on it is good practice to give all students who struggle with the spellings of number words the following numbers on a card, which they can keep with them to use when required.

1	One	11	Eleven	30	Thirty
2	Two	12	Twelve	40	Forty
3	Three	13	Thirteen	50	Fifty
4	Four	14	Fourteen	60	Sixty
5	Five	15	Fifteen	70	Seventy
6	Six	16	Sixteen	80	Eighty
7	Seven	17	Seventeen	90	Ninety
8	Eight	18	Eighteen	100	Hundred
9	Nine	19	Nineteen	1000	Thousand
10	Ten	20	twenty	1 000 000	Million

Odd and even

Students may have difficulty understanding and remembering just what the words 'odd' and 'even' mean. It is important to use different strategies to try to give them confidence to cope with questions that either use specific odd and even numbers or recognize the sequence of odd and even patterns. If possible, it is a good idea to use everyday life situations to link number and number sequences so that students are better able to understand. Usually this can lead to students having a good chance of remembering and making sense of these numbers later. Some strategies used successfully are on page 16:

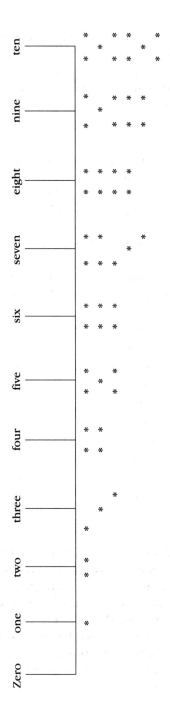

Figure 2.

- Starting with one cube we imagine that this is the student on his own. We discuss that as he has no one to play with it could be described as a lonely situation, therefore we shall recognize the number 1 as an 'odd' number. Selecting another cube we place it alongside the first cube and talk about the second cube as a friend who has come to play making an 'even' number. Once a third cube or pretend friend appears it is easy to see that we have two friends and an odd one left so the number three is an 'odd' number leaving one of the children to play on his own. Students seem to relate to this situation as it happens every day in the playground. Once they have the idea of having a friend and making a pair to make an even number or there being someone who is left on their own when the pairs have all been made, making an odd number, we can then start to look at the patterns that odd and even numbers make.

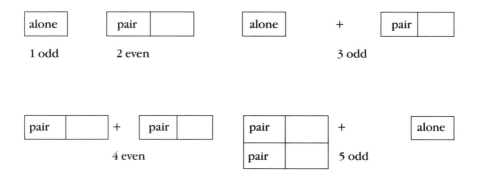

- Cubes can be arranged on the table as two towers, so that we begin with 1 cube as the base for the first tower. (Say aloud '1 is odd'.) The second cube is the base start for the second tower we are going to build. (Say '2 is even'.) The third cube is added to the first cube of the first tower and students can easily see the one is higher than the other and the towers are not of equal heights therefore they are odd. (Say aloud '3 is odd'.) As we progress, we see quite clearly the difference between odd and even numbers by looking at the different heights of the towers as cubes are added; always follow up the physical building with describing the number as odd or even. Using numbers up to 20, then 30, discuss and look at the differing sizes of the towers. Some students like to use different coloured blocks to show odd and even; allow them to do this as it reinforces the concept. Students are then able to record this experiment by drawing and colouring the towers in their books, clearly marking both the numbers of cubes used and also whether the number is odd or even.

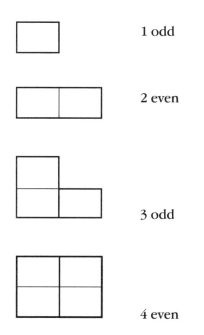

1 odd

2 even

3 odd

4 even

- Use weighing scales or simply hands and arms to be a pretend balance to show how one cube (or one of anything practical) makes the balance uneven. Talk about how an odd number makes the scales look and then see how by putting a cube on the other side of the scales or in the other hand will 'even up' the balance. This can be done as before, showing first odd and then even numbers and considering how the balance is affected by them.

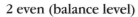

1 odd (balance not level)   2 even (balance level)

8 Using a 1–100 number square discuss the practical experiments that you have been doing and then decide how you can visually represent the patterns on the square. Perhaps you will colour all odd numbers and leave the even numbers plain; using colour in some way shows how the odd and even numbers appear as straight lines on the square. This then can be put up on the wall as a visual and constant reminder to the student (see over).

1	2	3	4	5	6	7	8	9	10
11	12	13	14	15	16	17	18	19	20
21	22	23	24	25	26	27	28	29	30
31	32	33	34	35	36	37	38	39	40
41	42	43	44	45	46	47	48	49	50
51	52	53	54	55	56	57	58	59	60
61	62	63	64	65	66	67	68	69	70
71	72	73	74	75	76	77	78	79	80
81	82	83	84	85	86	87	88	89	90
91	92	93	94	95	96	97	98	99	100

Seeing, chanting and rhyming

Dyslexic students like to look and recognize number patterns, so a helpful oral exercise can be done starting with 2, (and adding on two each time) following the numbers on the 1–100 square so that students can link their chant with the even numbers on the square. Sometimes students will know or make up a rhyme that will help them to remember the odd or even numbers.

e.g.   Just remember what you are taught!
         Even numbers end in 2, 4, 6, 8 or nought.

         1, 3 and 5 are odd numbers that's true
         Must try to remember that 7 and 9 are odd too!

Looking for the last digit

Once a pupil is happy with the idea of odd and even numbers it is important to talk about recognizing them quickly and easily. Students need to be aware which is the last digit in a number, in fact they need to know that it is the last digit which 'ends' a number. (Often because of their difficulty with left and right, before and after and first and last they do not realize that the final digit is the one on the right of a number.) Time needs to be spent on recognizing this important fact and once they are secure in this the teacher can proceed to say that if a number ends in 0, 2, 4, 6 or 8, regardless of the size of the number, then that number is even. Conversely any number that ends in 1,3,5,7 or 9 will be odd. We have found that many students will need an exercise to practise this, possibly highlighting the digit that ends a number and stating whether or not it is odd or even.

Highlight the last digit in the following numbers:

(a) 12   (b) 17   (c) 28   (d) 45
(e) 81   (f) 103   (g) 226   (h) 578

Dividing by two

If a pupil is asked to say what he knows about odd and even numbers before any teaching on this topic, he will probably reply glibly that an even number is a number that can be divided by two, without having any understanding of the implications of this distinction. However, after having worked through this section, students are able to see in their mind's eye the patterns of odd and even numbers and be able to understand whether a number can be divided by two. They will usually relate this new idea by looking to see if the number ends in 0, 2, 4, 6 or 8 and make the connection.

Number squares

If students become really interested in odd and even numbers it is possible to explore more advanced patterns by discussion and completion of number squares. They will be most likely to understand if the teacher demonstrates pictorially, with 'arrays' (diagrams in columns) of coloured shapes, crosses or, if preferred, 3D blocks.

We can ask what happens when:

- two even numbers are added   (always results in an even
  together ?   number total)

When you add two even numbers, the result will always be an even number, as the two even formations join together.

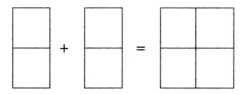

The following table is one that can be used to show the results when different even numbers are added together. Students might like to fill in a blank table to show these results.

+	2	4	6	8	10
2	4	6	8	10	12
4	6	8	10	12	14
6	8	10	12	14	16
8	10	12	14	16	18
10	12	14	16	18	20

- two odd numbers are added together?

(always results in an even number total)

When you add two odd numbers, the result will always be an even number, as the two odd ones combine.

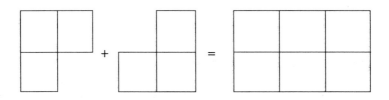

The following table is one that can be used to show the results when different odd numbers are added together. Students might like to fill in a blank table to show these results.

+	1	3	5	7	9
1	2	4	6	8	10
3	4	6	8	10	12
5	6	8	10	12	14
7	8	10	12	14	16
9	10	12	14	16	18

- an odd and even number are added together?

(always results in an odd number total)

Only when you add an odd number to an even one will the answer be odd.

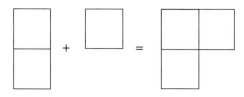

The following table is one that can be used to show the results when a variety of odd and even numbers are added to together. Students might like to fill in a blank table to show these results.

+	2	4	6	8	10
1	3	5	7	9	11
3	5	7	9	11	13
5	7	9	11	13	15
7	9	11	13	15	17
9	11	13	15	17	19

- two even numbers are multiplied?

(always results in an even number total)

×	2	4	6	8	10
2	4	8	12	16	20
4	8	16	24	32	40
6	12	24	36	48	60
8	16	32	48	64	80
10	20	40	60	80	100

- two odd numbers are multiplied?

(always results in an odd number total)

×	1	3	5	7	9
1	1	3	5	7	9
3	3	9	15	21	27
5	5	15	25	35	45
7	7	21	35	49	63
9	9	27	45	63	81

- An odd and even number are   (always results in an even
  multiplied?   number total)

×	2	4	6	8	10
1	2	4	6	8	10
3	6	12	18	24	30
5	10	20	30	40	50
7	14	28	42	56	70
9	18	36	54	72	90

As shown, we can make odd and even numbers accessible to all. It can be time consuming, but the skills students develop while exploring these numbers enable them to recognize important patterns and sequences, thus making vital connections as they gain in mathematical knowledge.

Pascal's Triangle

It is not essential to include this, but dyslexics often enjoy patterns. In Pascal's Triangle each number in a row is the sum of the two either side of it in the row above, forming an inverted triangle. Now students can complete the next row down, and even the row after that, if the teacher copies the diagram. Having done so, they can look at some interesting patterns. If they start on the righthand side with the diagonal sequences, the first two rows are easy to understand (11111 etc. and 12345 etc.). How does the next row go? (Answers on page 26.)

```
                          1
                    1           1
                1       2           1
            1       3       3           1
        1       4       6       4           1
    1       5       10      10      5           1
```

Once the pattern is seen and understood, students may begin to point out other interesting patterns.

Basic codes used in mathematics

As we said earlier, dyslexics have difficulty in rote learning. They cannot easily memorize the various codes that are used to express mathematical concepts, e.g. the plus and equals signs or the significance of the line between the numerator and denominator in a fraction; equally they do not absorb the algorithms for mathematical operations such as long multi-plication.

Consequently they must fully understand the reasoning in the system and processes behind it all, and the best way to explain these is for them to use multisensory aids to perform basic operations before recording them with fingers and other symbols.

The Four Operational Rules

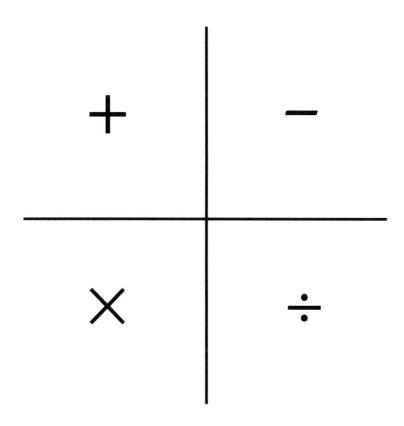

Place Value

The columns we use in the number system are not of equal value. They go up increasingly in status from right to left. The pupil might like to think of them as increasingly grand houses, starting with a kennel, something like this:

Then they could move on to playing with multisensory blocks of some kind. The great advantage of using multisensory blocks is that the 'tens' are spatially ten times the size of the 'units' and the 'hundreds' are ten times the size of the 'tens' and so on, which represents in a very vivid way the numerical relationship between the 'columns' in which numbers are entered. It is therefore a very good idea to give the pupil the opportunity to see and feel these relationships for himself. As long as plain coloured blocks are used they will not seem childish. If it is quite impossible to obtain a set of blocks, it is possible to use two-dimensional diagrams of squares – or even money, but here the existence of other intermediate coin values may obscure the base ten system. However the money system can be explained thereafter, and practice given in giving change.

Use of Multisensory Blocks

We recommend an informal approach with the blocks so the pupil will play with them, relax and want to become involved with any exercises where he can use the blocks to problem-solve. Use the blocks as follows:

• First read any accompanying leaflet supplied with the blocks and study how to use them. An informal approach is best to put the pupil at ease, with both teacher and pupil handling the blocks. The pupil should be encouraged to talk freely about them and what he thinks their purpose might be.

- There should be unstructured 'trading', with the pupil having complete access to the materials and being encouraged to verbalize his thoughts about the operations he is performing. This is very important because at this stage symbols are not used to record at all.
- Confidence with the materials having been achieved, the pupil can move on to the computations covered in the following sections in this book on the four operations, continuing to 'trade', working with the blocks on a large sheet of paper marked out in columns for hundreds, tens, units and lines at the bottom for the answer.

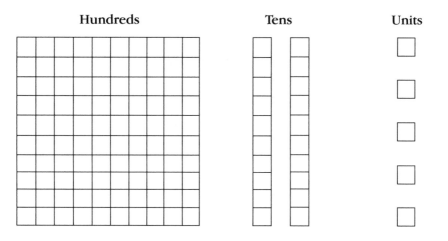

The pupil should all the time say aloud what he is doing, as is recommended in Mary Kibel's chapter 'Linking language to action' in *Dyslexia and Mathematics* (Kibel 1992). There is also a multimedia calculator now available (Flynn, 1997) in which the user can operate the mouse to do a sum with 'blocks' while a voice describes what is being done. However it is important, as Kibel points out, that the pupil himself shall describe what he is doing. (References to both these are to be found at the end of this chapter.)

- The sums can now be recorded in numerals after the operation. Particular care should be taken with the carrying figure so that it is clearly written and its positioning does not interfere with the other digits. The function of the carrying figure in recording a 'trading' operation must be fully understood. (Usual practice at the student's school should be followed, with the tutor correcting in the student's work only what is unclear and confuses other parts of the sum, but the pupil must understand it.)
- The teacher will be able to tell when the pupil no longer needs the apparatus, because the pupil will discard it himself.

The Four Operational Rules

Why these are called 'rules' is not quite clear, but it is perhaps typical of a rote-learning approach that we want to avoid with dyslexics.

The pupil must fully understand the processes of addition, subtraction, multiplication and division that he is going to use, and how they are related to each other. In discussing these informally with the pupil it is desirable to have multisensory aids available to add, subtract, multiply and divide physically. Beads will do for this, or beans. Each process is expounded more fully in the next four Chapters, which deal with them all singly and give practice exercises.

Answers to Pascal's Triangle (p. 22)

The next line down will be

1	6	15	20	15	6	1

The first diagonal sequence is   1   1   1   1   1 etc.

The second diagonal sequence is   1   2   3   4   5 etc.

The third diagonal sequence is   1   3   6   10   15 etc.
(with the *differences* between the numbers increasing by one each time).

The fourth diagonal sequence is   1   4   10   20   [35]etc.
The *differences* between the numbers are: 3   6   10   15 etc.

This is the same as the third diagonal sequence above. So it is the *differences between the differences* which increase by 1 each time.

There are other more sophisticated patterns in Pascal's Triangle, e.g. to do with possible combinations, but this will do for a start!

Chapter 4
Addition

ADDITION

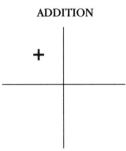

Teachers' notes

The first kind of addition that children learn is the summing up of separate objects that can be counted, and using blocks will have trained them in this.

They must then understand that addition can also be done along a continuous line where a scale has been imposed, giving equal sized pieces, as in measurement of length or width and temperature on a thermometer. This sort of addition is most easily demonstrated by a number line, which can be turned up vertically where this is more relevant, and different scales written in. Both sorts of sums are illustrated in our exercises.

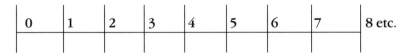

You may wish first to discuss the symbol for addition and what words are used for it, see page 29.

27

When working the sums on paper, it is useful to know that in addition the numbers involved can be added in any order without making any difference, e.g. 3 + 4 + 7 is the same as 7 + 4 + 3 or 3 + 7 + 4. This is true also of multiplication, but not of subtraction and division.

The name for this is the *Commutative Principle*, but it is not necessary for your students to learn this term, as long as they understand the principle.

This is useful, because it is sometimes easier to add certain numbers first. In the above sum, adding 3 and 7 first gives 10; then it is easy to add 4.

Students could try adding different strings of small numbers to look for the easiest way. They are less likely to make mistakes if they do this.

They also need to practise adding small numbers together, including ones crossing the ten division (e.g. 7 + 4), so that elementary 'number facts' come easily to them.

A carrying number at the top of a column indicates the number of 'longs' that the added 'units' have added up to; these have to be added in when adding the next column. Refer back to the concrete materials or a pictorial form of them (you can get stamps for this). The teacher needs to point out that the carrying number is not always '1'! When there are more than two numbers to add, it can be more:

$$
\begin{array}{r}
{}^{1} \\
29 \\
+\,34 \\
\hline
63
\end{array}
\qquad
\begin{array}{r}
{}^{2} \\
29 \\
34 \\
+\,58 \\
\hline
121
\end{array}
$$

Quick estimations with rounded off numbers

Round off to the nearer 10, add up the digits and put a 0 in the answer

Examples

        14 + 32
        rounded off is 10 + 30
        1 + 3 is 4, add 0 is 40
        (exact answer is 46)

        35 + 213
        rounded off is 40 + 210
        4 + 21 is 25, add 0 is 250.
        (exact answer is 248)

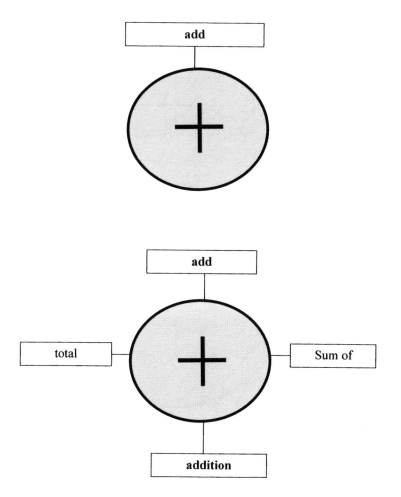

The addition symbol

- Draw a circle and ask the student to put the addition symbol in the centre.
- Colour the circle with a favourite colour.
- Discuss what the symbol represents. Talk about the sort of answers you would expect if you add together e.g. 7 and 2.
- Do an estimate and then use apparatus to find an accurate answer. Discuss that the answer is always bigger than either number involved.

Single symbol for addition

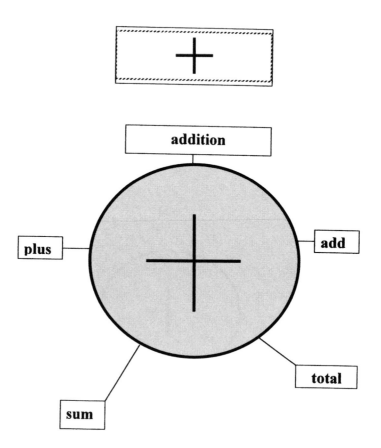

- Ask what words he would use to describe the symbol, and then put those words around the symbol so that it can be put on a wall for constant review.
- Try the following questions to see if he can read and understand the words and can tell you what kind of calculation he would do to find a solution.

> Add together 5 and 11.
> What is the sum of 5 and 1?
> What is the total of 3, 6 and 8?

Examples of Addition

Estimate then calculate accurately
Use a 1–100 square and/or a number line (Can you spot patterns in (a) and
(b)?)

(a)
10+6	10+1	10+9	10+3
10+16	10+11	10+19	10+13
10+22	10+52	10+31	10+87

(b)
1+5	1+15	1+25	1+35
2+8	2+18	2+28	2+58
3+7	3+17	3+27	3+67
4+5	4+25	4+65	4+95

(c)
| 6+11 | 5+23 | 7+31 | 8+40 |
| 2+17 | 8+19 | 3+12 | 5+16 |

(d)

| 12 | 20 | 32 | 47 |
| +25 | +46 | +50 | +21 |

| 17 | 29 | 50 | 63 |
| +22 | +30 | +37 | +14 |

(e)

| 58 | 63 | 29 | 24 |
| +35 | +18 | +46 | +58 |

| 66 | 73 | 57 | 25 |
| +30 | +17 | +26 | +55 |

(f)

| 106 | 236 | 317 | 236 |
| +289 | +335 | +174 | +334 |

(g)

| 542 | 623 | 395 | 167 |
| +269 | +184 | +305 | +484 |

Answers are on page 142

Magic Squares

A magic square is one in which the numbers whether added upwards, downwards, across or diagonally **give the same answer, which is called the total**.

(1) Complete the following magic square using only the numbers 4, 5 and 6 to give a | total of 15 |

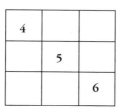

4		
	5	
		6

(2) What is the total of the magic square below?
Complete this magic square using numbers: 1, 2, 3, 7, 8 and 9 only once.

4		
	5	
		6

(3) Look at this square.   What is its total?
Is it magic?

11	4	9
6	8	10
7	12	5

Yes	No

(4) Add 5 to each number in question 3 and fill up this square.
    Is it still magic?

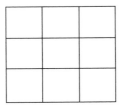

Yes	No

(5) Try to complete the following Magic Square (use a calculator).
    First find the total of the diagonal.

Total: [ ]

15		13
	12	
11		

Answers to Magic Squares

(1)

4	6	5
6	5	4
5	4	6

(2)

4	9	2
3	5	7
8	1	6

(3)

Total = 24   No.3 is a magic square

(4)

16	9	14
11	13	15
12	17	10

No.4 is a magic square

(5)

15	8	13
10	12	14
11	16	9

Chapter 5
Subtraction

SUBTRACTION

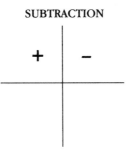

Subtraction is the opposite of addition.

Children learn it first as the removal of separate objects.

Then they must understand that, like addition it can be done on a continuous line with a scale imposed, as on a number line.

But they must also learn to see subtraction as a way of showing the *difference* in size between e.g. two rectangles marked off in squares, one having 8 squares and one having 6, or two lines, one 10 centimetres long and one 7 centimetres long, etc. There will be practice examples of all three kinds.

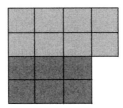

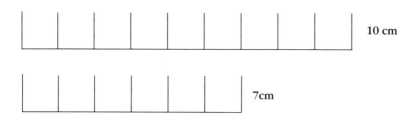

You may first want to discuss the symbol for subtraction and the words that are used for it, see page 38.

It is very important that they realize that subtraction cannot be done in any direction. (It is not commutative.) You cannot just pick out the larger number and take the smaller one away! For instance if your bank balance is £5 and you draw out £6 (5–6) , you are 'in the red' (Your balance is –£1). You cannot just take 5 from 6 instead and say you still have £1 in the bank!

They should practise doing small subtraction sums (which they can check with beans or coins), including ones that go across the tens dividing line, e.g. 15–8, 12–6, 24–7 etc., always checking by adding afterwards.

In subtraction they will sometimes have to 'borrow' from the next column, and they need to understand how to record this by reducing the top number in the next column. In the first sum below 10 must be borrowed to make 14, so that 9 can be subtracted, and then the 3 in the left-hand column becomes 2. In the second sum again 10 is borrowed to make 14, and the 5 in the left-hand column becomes 4. It is best to cross out the altered numbers and put in the new numbers.

$$
\begin{array}{r}
\overset{2}{\cancel{3}}4 \\
-\ 29 \\
\hline
5
\end{array}
\qquad
\begin{array}{r}
\overset{4}{\cancel{5}}4 \\
-\ 28 \\
\hline
26
\end{array}
$$

Make sure he understands this process, referring back to the multi-sensory blocks, or pictures of them.

Try the following question to see if he can read and understand the words and can tell you what kind of calculation he would do to find a solution:

What is the answer when you subtract 6 from 11?
What is the difference between 13 and 8?

Using a number line to do subtraction

In real life situations such as shopping or giving someone change, it is rare for subtraction calculations to be done because most people 'add on' in order to count up to the total sum given. Using a number line allows students to do this easily. They can see the line, recognize where the number they are dealing with will come, and add on in easy numbers to the value they are subtracting from.

e.g. Take 7 from 16

Choose an appropriate number line

```
|   |   |   |   |   |   |   |   |   |   |   |
0   2   4   6   8   10  12  14  16  18  20  22
```

See where 7 comes and put it between 6 and 8
Mark where 16 comes on the line.
Count on from 7 to 8 = 1
Count in 2s up to 16 = 8
1+8 = 9

e.g. Subtract 24 from 57
Choose an appropriate number line

```
|    |    |    |    |    |    |    |    |
0  5  10  15  20  25  30  35  40  45  50  55  60  65  70
```

Find where 24 will be and put a mark just to the left of 25.
Find where 57 will be and put a mark.
Count on from 24 to 25   = 1
Count in 5s up to 55   = 30
Count from 55 to 57   = 2
The answer is 1+30 +2   = 33

Estimations for subtraction

Round off to the nearest 10, subtract the digits and put a 0 in the answer.

e.g. 68 – 17

Rounded off is 70 – 20
7 – 2 is 5.
Estimated answer is 50
(Exact answer is 51)

e.g. 475 – 53
Rounded off is 480 – 50
48 – 5 is 43
Estimated answer is 430
(Exact answer is 422)

The subtraction symbol

- Draw a circle and ask the student to put the subtraction symbol in the centre.
- Colour the circle with a favourite colour.

Symbol for Subtraction

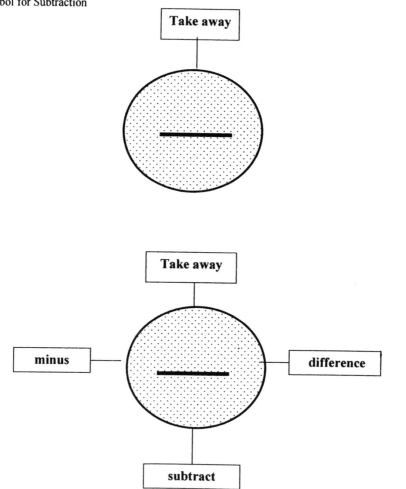

Single symbol for subtraction

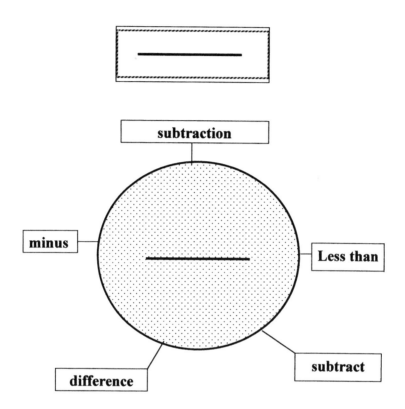

- Discuss what the symbol represents. Talk about the sort of answers you would expect if you take 2 from 4 or 3 from 6, etc.
- Do an estimate and then use apparatus to find an accurate answer. Discuss that the answer is always smaller.
- Ask what words he would use to describe the symbol and then put those words around the symbol. If possible make a wall chart with the symbol plus the words he associated with that symbol so that it can be put on a wall for constant review.

Examples of Subtraction

Estimate, then calculate accurately
Use a 1–100 square and/or a number line (Can you spot patterns in (a), (b)
and (c)?)

(a)

10 – 2	10 – 4	10 – 6	10 – 8
6 – 1	16 – 1	26 – 1	36 – 1
22 – 10	45 – 10	56 – 10	80 – 10

(b)

20 – 11	20 – 12	20 – 13	20 – 14
14 – 9	24 – 9	64 – 9	94 – 9

(c)

11 – 4	21 – 4	51 – 4	81 – 4
9 – 7	19 – 7	39 – 7	89 – 7

(d)

25	46	58	44
−12	−23	−17	−22

(e)

55	63	96	77
− 38	−19	−27	−48

(f)

66	71	52	88
−29	−17	−16	−19

(g)

269	536	437	873
−134	−115	−225	−531

(h)

582	663	395	967
−257	−234	−387	−218

(i)

436	689	525	736
−263	−199	−370	−151

(j)

517	703	601	900
−348	−114	−387	−218

Answers on page 142

Chapter 6
Multiplication

MULTIPLICATION

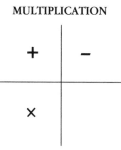

Multiplication is addition repeated several times by adding the same number.

e.g. 4×3 is the same as $3 + 3 + 3 + 3$, that is 3 added 4 times.

It is useful to know the number facts from 'multiplication tables' so that simple multiplications like this can be done immediately and quickly. Because multiplication is a form of addition it can be done in any direction just the same as addition, and this helps with getting to know the multiplication number facts – e.g. since 8×3 is the same as 3×8, if you know the answer to one you know the answer to the other.

This saves a lot of memorizing in multiplication tables.

We have a section on Multiplication Tables following this, which gives various ways of learning these useful facts.

You may want to discuss the symbol for multiplication first and what words are used for it. see page 44.

(If your pupil has done algebra you can point out that you do not need a $\times$ sign for '3 times y' etc. 3y means '3 times y'. If you did this with digits alone it would not do – 33 does *not* mean 3 times 3.)

41

Using number lines

Once students are used to doing number lines they will be able to put multiples of numbers on them, possibly using colours for different number groups. If they are working with 3s, the they can mark off groups of 3s on the number line. When asked what 5×3 is they will count up the groups to see the answer 15.

e.g.

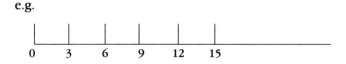

Students can use number lines to show the multiples until they feel confident to work them out independently, without using the number lines. (Conversely they will be able to use their multiple number lines to do division, so that when asked how many 3s are in 15, they will be able to count the groups in the other direction to see the answer is 5.)

Estimation with multiplication

As dyslexic students are constantly troubled with multiplication, to ask them to estimate multiplication sums often falls on deaf ears, and they will try to use the exact numbers to find an answer. However if they are shown with careful rounding off to either the nearest 10 or 100, or to an easy number, that there is a way to be fairly accurate, then they are willing to try. It is important to emphasize that the calculation must be one that they can easily do, which means the student must use numbers that he understands the value of and is able to manipulate to reach an answer, using a method in which he feels confidence. As can be seen in the following examples, sometimes it is necessary to start again, especially if the strategy leaves us with numbers that are far too difficult to manage quickly and easily, which is one of the main advantages of doing estimations.

To multiply using estimations, round off to the nearest 10 or 100, depending on the question and the size of the numbers involved, add up the 0's and put them in the answer, then multiply the remaining digits.

Example 26×14
Round off the numbers (nearer 10) 30×10
Add the 0's   put 00 in the answer
$3 \times 1 = 3$ put 3 in the answer
Estimated answer is 300 (exact answer is 364)

If a more accurate estimate is required
Round off to the nearer 5 25×15
$25 \times 10 = 250$
$25 \times 5 = 125$ (half of the above) Add these
Estimated answer is 375 (exact answer is 364)

Example 337×79
Round off the numbers to nearer 10 340×80
Add up the 0's   put 00 in the answer
34×8

This is too difficult

Start again
Round off the numbers (nearer 100) 300×100
Add up the 0's   put 0000 in answer
$3 \times 1 = 3$
Estimated answer is 30,000 (exact answer is 26,623)

If a more accurate estimate is required
Round off the numbers (nearer 100 or 10) 300×80
Add up the 0's   put 000 in answer
$3 \times 8 = 24$
Estimated answer is 24,000 (exact answer is 26,623)

The multiplication symbol

- Draw a circle and ask the student to put the multiplication symbol in the centre.
- Colour the circle with a favourite colour.
- Discuss what the symbol represents. Talk about the sort of answers you would expect if you multiply 4 by 2.
- Do an estimate and then use apparatus to find an exact answer, discuss that the answer is always bigger than either number involved.
- Ask the student what words he would use to describe the symbol and then put those words around the symbol. If possible make a wall chart with the symbol plus the words that he associated with that symbol so that it can be put on a wall for constant review.
- Try the following questions to see if he can tell you what kind of calculation he would do to find a solution:
  - What is 2 times 3?
  - What is the product of 3 and 3?
  - Multiply 4 by 2.

Symbol for multiplication

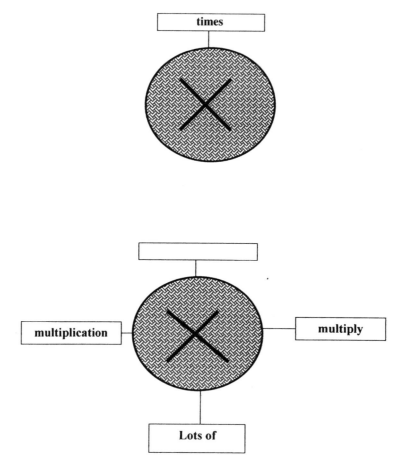

Single symbol for multiplication

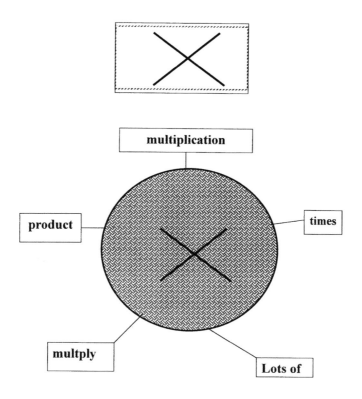

Long Multiplication

e.g. 52×46

Make a card with on one side – blank on the reverse side

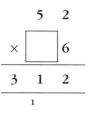
      multiply by the 6
      use the blank side to cover the 4 in 46

```
        5   2           multiply by the 40
                        put a 0 in the answer
    ×   4  | 0↓ |

        3   1   2

    2   0   8   0

    2   3   9   2
```

- The card reminds students that first they multiply by the 6
- By using the card with the 0 and arrow pointing downwards students are reminded that they need to put a nought in the answer before multiplying by the 4.

Chinese Lattice Method of Long Multiplication

Problem   786 × 34
Estimate   800 × 30   =   24,000 (approx.)

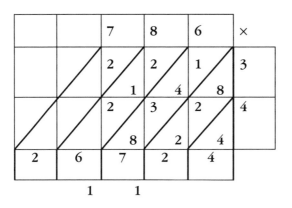

- Use 0.7 cm squared paper
- Draw in the red lattice lines
- Take one digit from the top number 786 and multiply it by a digit from 34 on the right hand side. Continue until all the 3 digits in 786 will have been multiplied by both the 30 and the 4 from the right hand side.
- In each square the answer is recorded with the units under the red lattice line and the tens above the lattice line.
- Then starting with the lattice line on the right add up all numbers between the adjacent bold lines, and write the answer at the bottom as follows:

- 1st line   = 4
- 2nd line   = 8 + 2 + 2   = 12   2 down, carry the 1
- 3rd line   = 1 + 4 + 3 + 8 + 1   = 17   7 down, carry the 1
- 4th line   = 2 + 1 + 2 + 1   = 6
- 5th line   = 2

The answer is 126,724

Examples of Multiplication

Estimate then calculate accurately. Use a Table square, 1–100 square and/or a number line.

(a) 2×2 4×2 10×2 5×2
         3×5 6×5 4×5 8×5

(b) 10×6 10×4 10×8 10×2
         20×3 20×2 20×4 20×1
         16×0 58×0 97×0 33×0

(c)   24   33   12   10
         $\times 2$ $\times 1$ $\times 4$ $\times 6$

(d)   52   40   31   40
         $\times 2$ $\times 3$ $\times 7$ $\times 9$

(e)   55   63   96   77
         $\times 8$ $\times 9$ $\times 7$ $\times 6$

(f)   220   101   200   130
         $\times 4$ $\times 7$ $\times 2$ $\times 3$

(g)   260   506   407   870
         $\times 2$ $\times 5$ $\times 9$ $\times 8$

(h) 12×10 22×10 62×10 92×10
         12×100 22×100 62×100 92×100

           82   63   395   967
         $\times 10$ $\times 10$ $\times 10$ $\times 10$

(i)   36   68   55   97
         $\times 63$ $\times 14$ $\times 37$ $\times 92$

(j)   517   703   601   900
         $\times 69$ $\times 11$ $\times 87$ $\times 21$

Answers are on page 146

Multiplication Tables

Instant recall of multiplication facts is a useful skill as it can reduce the time needed to do both written and mental calculations. Almost all dyslexic students will tell you that they cannot remember their 'tables'; in fact older students often will say that this poor memory with multiplication tables has caused them to fail in mathematics, and indeed resulted in a loss of self-esteem and confidence which in turn has affected all areas of their lives. How can we as teachers of younger students try to help these students before this 'failing' takes place?

We need to know that 'tables' are multiplication tables, sets of multiplication facts and it is important to realize that students need to know only the individual facts. While saying each table through is a traditional way of helping students remember these facts, for many dyslexic students who cannot remember the sequences involved with each multiplication table, saying tables becomes an almost impossible, daunting task. Students can be told that there are many different ways of learning these tables, and rote chanting (which most dyslexic students cannot do) is not the only one.

There are audio-tapes and CDs and these can be used with students who find them useful. Computer programs that encourage quick, decisive answers with tables can be extremely beneficial, allowing students to succeed or fail quietly and to make improvement without the rest of the class knowing. Students can then move on to higher, maybe faster, levels so that their skills in this difficult task can improve and their progress will be clearly charted on the computer. Printouts can be obtained that can be used, if they wish, to show their improvement to others, even the teacher.

Beads that are strung in specific sets of colours, e.g. 3 red, 3 blue, 3 red, etc. can help with tables. 'Sumthings' are beads on threads, which can be made to order to assist with all multiplication tables.

Several methods that we have used successfully are described here so that you may use whichever you find that will assist the particular learning style of your student.

The answers in these tables are 'multiples', and the numbers that you multiply are called 'factors'. (This is worth mentioning if students have already come across factors – Highest Common Factor and Lowest Common Factor. 'Common' means 'belonging to all' or 'shared', as a bit of 'common' is a bit of land shared with the general public.)

It is as well to establish understanding of 'even' and 'odd' numbers first (see Chapter 3, 'Understanding number'). In an even–numbered table

(2,4,6, etc.) the answers will all be even numbers. Try this out with 'arrays' as with the addition sums.

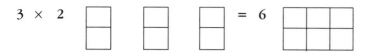

In an odd- numbered table **half** the answers will be even numbers, that is, when you are multiplying the odd number by the even one.

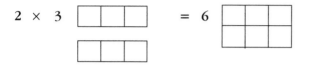

Only when both numbers are odd will the answer in a table be an odd number! It will not 'pair off'.

Any number multiplied by 0 is 0. 5 × 0 'means there are no 5s'.

Multiplication, like Addition, can be done starting with either number. So if you know 5 × 4, you also know 4 × 5, and so on. This cuts the work of learning table facts by half. (Keep reminding students of this. If they hesitate over 4 × 7 in the 7 times table, did they know 7 × 4 in the 4 times table?). Saying tables aloud is not necessary unless it helps certain students; the object is to learn the facts.

Using an 'array'

Table sum answers (multiples) can be illustrated by arrays, as we have shown earlier. Students may well understand them better represented in this spatial way, and constructed by themselves, especially if they are more able spatially. A whole table can be represented by arrays (choose only a low-numbered one to array or you will run out of space). Then the sums can be recorded in symbols beside the array afterwards.

Patterns in tables

The answers in each table will also make a distinctive pattern on a 1–100 square, and this may interest the spatially-minded. The 3 times table looks like this:

1	2	3	4	5	6	7	8	9	10
11	12	13	14	15	16	17	18	19	20
21	22	23	24	25	26	27	28	29	30
31	32	33	34	35	36	37	38	39	40
41	42	43	44	45	46	47	48	49	50
51	52	53	54	55	56	57	58	59	60
61	62	63	64	65	66	67	68	69	70
71	72	73	74	75	76	77	78	79	80
81	82	83	84	85	86	87	88	89	90
91	92	93	94	95	96	97	98	99	100

A 100 number square will be found in the Appendix (A2, p. 132)

Two Times Table

- Start with twos, as many students will not feel threatened with this low number. Using blocks make up the two times table up to 8 saying as you do so 2, 4, 6, 8.

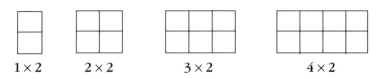

1×2 $\qquad$ 2×2 $\qquad$ 3×2 $\qquad$ 4×2

- Draw the pattern made and colour in the arrays, again saying 2, 4, 6, 8.
- With the pattern in front of you walk 4 steps and clap, saying as you do so 2, 4, 6, 8.
- Look to see how far you have walked when you reach 8.
- Continue in this way building up the table, drawing the patterns, colouring them in and walking a little further until you have reached 20.
- Once your student is confident with the pattern of this table he can try

saying the answers, e.g. 2 and putting up one finger at the same time so that when you ask 'How many twos are there in 2?' he will know the answer by counting how many fingers he has put up. Proceeding in this manner putting up another finger each time a 2 is added, your student will begin to see that when he says 16 and he has put 8 fingers up then there are 8 twos in 16. (This method may be used with any table and is especially helpful if the students and teacher are able to 'walk' at the same time.)

Ten Times Table

Count fingers to make sure your student knows that he has got ten fingers.

- Ask him to see if he knows what 2 tens are, possibly by putting your hands alongside his to help. Say 10, 20 and see if he will add 30, 40 and so on. If he does so then practise together counting aloud up to 100. Each time a number is said make your student shake all ten fingers to make sure that he knows that he is adding on 10 each time.
- Once he has become confident with this try walking and clapping saying the numbers aloud. Look again to see how far you have walked across the room by the time you have reached 100.
- Use the finger method described in the last section of 2 times table with 10s.

Five Times table

- By looking at just one hand, count fingers and recognize 5.
- Many students like to look at the pattern of five as shown on all playing cards, often accepting only this as the pattern of 5.

```
        *           *
             *
        *           *
```

- Count in fives 5, 10, 15, 20 using a hand movement each time; students can usually say this table easily.
- Colour in the pattern on the 1–100 square, commenting on the straight line pattern.
- Once your student is confident with the pattern of this table he can try saying the answers e.g. 5 and putting up one finger at the same time so that when you ask 'How many fives are there in 5?' he will know what the answer is by counting how many fingers he has put up. Proceed in this manner putting up another finger each time a 5 is added so that your student will begin to see that when he says 25 and he has put 5 fingers up then there are 5 fives in 25.

- With the pattern in front of you walk 5 steps and clap saying as you do so 5, 10, 15, 20, 25.
- Look to see how far you have walked when you reach 25.

Continue in this way building up the table, drawing the patterns, colouring them in and walking a little further until you have reached 50.

Three Times Table

- Look at one finger to see the three sections (segments, pieces) there, count them and say 3. Count how many sections in two fingers, then three fingers. say 3, 6, 9.
- Put multicubes into threes and count those.
- Arrange a 'sumthing' into threes, or better still have one made with different colours to show the three times table.
- Colour in the pattern on the 1–100 square, commenting on the diagonal line pattern. Note that the answers are alternately odd and even numbers.

Once your student is confident with the pattern of this table he can try saying the answers e.g. 3 and putting up one finger at the same time so that when you ask 'How many threes are there in 3?' he will know the answer is one by counting how many fingers he has put up, reinforced for this table with the sections in each individual finger. By putting up another finger each time a 3 is added your student will begin to see that when he says 12 and he has put 4 fingers up then there are 4 threes in 12.

With the pattern in front of you walk and clap 4 steps, saying as you do so 3, 6, 9, 12.

Look to see how far you have walked when you reach 12.

Continue in this way building up the table, drawing the patterns, colouring them in and walking a little further until you have reached 30.

Four Times Table

- Count in fours up to twelve looking at the 1–100 square.
- Say 4, 8, 12 putting up a finger each time so that the students will understand that $3 \times 4 = 12$.
- Gradually build up the table and colour in the pattern on the 1–100 square.
- Look then at the pattern of the table noticing the final digits in the numbers: 4 8 12 16 20 24 28 32 36 40

Once students recognize the 4, 8, 2, 6, 0 endings they will recognise by the final digits numbers that are in the 4 times table.

Nine Times Table

Once students begin to grasp counting in nines show them the trick way of writing out the table. Writing numbers from 0 to 9 in a column, start at the top with 0 down to 9 then complete the second column by starting at the bottom with 0 and writing digits up to 9. Then look to see that you have written out the whole of the table correctly.

column 1	column 2	2 columns together
0	9	09
1	8	18
2	7	27
3	6	36
4	5	45
5	4	54
6	3	63
7	2	72
8	1	81
9	0	90

Show students the 9 times table on their fingers. The hardest part of this table is actually bending your fingers at the right time. If students have difficulty with this make some cardboard hands with fingers that bend so that students can use these instead. For this purpose a thumb counts as a finger.

Starting with left hand identify fingers 1-10, when we say:

1×9 Bend the first finger.
            Count the number of fingers not bent. Answer is 9
2×9 Bend the second finger.
            Finger to the left of the bent one has a value of 10, other 8 fingers are 8 units. Answer is 18
3×9 Bend the third finger.
            Fingers to the left of the bent one each have a value of $2 \times 10 = 20$, other 7 fingers are 7 units. Answer is 27
4×9 Bend the fourth finger.
            Fingers to the left of the bent one have a value of 30, other 6 fingers are 6 units. Answer is 36
5×9 Bend the fifth finger.
            Fingers to the left of the bent one have a value of 40, other 5 fingers are 5 units. Answer is 45

- Continue in this way for the whole of the table. Then practise until the student becomes fast and accurate.
- Colour the pattern of the table on the 1–100 square
- Look at the answers in the table, observe that if individual digits in each answer are added together they always make 9; talk about this.
- Later it is possible to investigate how to spot if a number is in the 9 times table. If we add the digits in a number and they make 9 then they are in the table. i.e. Is 24 in the table? $2 + 4 = 6$ so the answer is 'No'.

When students are beginning to grasp the different tables we usually follow the procedures mentioned for the earlier tables covering up to 5×6, 5×7, 5×8 we shall already have looked at 5×9 and 5×10, and then we will show them how to do finger tables for the rest.

i.e. 6×6, 7×6, 8×6, 9×6, 10×6
       6×7, 7×7, 8×7, 9×7, 10×7
       6×8, 7×8, 8×8, 9×8, 10×8
       6×9, 7×9, 8×9, 9×9, 10×9

How the computer can help

Students are keen to make table squares on the computer, which gives them a tidy copy and one that they may copy to give to their friends. They can make coloured ones or ones that pick out certain table patterns. It is also possible to show students that if they identify all the 'square numbers' i.e. 1×1, 2×2, 3×3, 4×4, 5×5, 6×6, 7×7, 8×8, 9×9, 10×10 in the square they have in fact drawn a line of symmetry through the square.

They can then fill in half the square, cut it out and fold it in half along the line of symmetry. They will be able to see clearly that the other half is an exact reflection of the one half that they have filled in, and in this way they will become aware that they need to know the facts in only half the table square because the other facts are just the same.

×	1	2	3	4	5	6	7	8	9	10
1	1	2	3	4	5	6	7	8	9	10
2		4	6	8	10	12	14	16	18	20
3			9	12	15	18	21	24	27	30
4				16	20	24	28	32	36	40
5					25	30	35	40	45	50
6						36	42	48	54	60
7							49	56	63	70
8								64	72	80
9									81	90
10										100

Chapter 7
Division

DIVISION

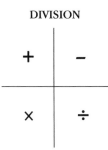

Division is a short way of continuous subtraction. If you divide 12 by 3, that is the same as if you took away 3 as many times as you can until you get to 0, and the answer is how many times it took to do it – in this case 4. If you have 16 tarts and you want to give 4 each, you can do so 4 times, i.e. to just 4 people.

If you had 17 tarts, there would be one left over, which we call 'the remainder'.

You may want to discuss the symbol for division first and the words that are used for it, see page 60.

Division is the reverse of multiplication.

Like subtraction, division cannot be done in either direction. Dividing 16 tarts among 4 people gives 4 whole tarts each. Dividing 4 tarts among 16 people gives them only a quarter each, quite a different matter. With a calculator you have to put the number you want to divide first, then press the division sign – **which means 'divided by'**, then the other number.

When you do a division sum on paper you work from left to right, unlike the other three processes – addition, subtraction, multiplication.

This is because then any 'remainders' in the lefthand column can be 'exchanged' for smaller currency in the next column, which you can divide in turn, like this:

$$
\begin{array}{r}
237 \\
\hline
^{1\,2} \\
4\,\big)\,9\overset{}{4}8
\end{array}
$$

Students might like to try working this sum from the right. When they get to the 9, they will find that they have a remainder of '1' (i.e. 100) which they cannot divide up at that stage without going back to the next two columns to the right!

There is a Fraction Section later, but if the student has already met fractions you can point out that the dividing line in a fraction indicates division. The top is 'divided by' the bottom. So 1 over 4 is 1 divided by 4 – a quarter. The division symbol itself has a dividing line with one dot above the line and one below.

Estimation with division

Almost all dyslexic students that we have taught have dreaded division as much as multiplication, so asking them to estimate with division just produced blank stares. However when we began to talk about different methods to do this, which could depend on them and their particular learning style, things improved. We found that once they are shown that there is a way to reach the answer by careful rounding off to the nearest 10 or 100 or by using easy numbers, they are willing to try. It is important to emphasize that the calculation must be one that is easy to do, which means that the student must use numbers that he understands the value of, and is able to manipulate using a method in which he feels confident. As can be seen in the following examples, sometimes it is necessary to *start again*, if the strategy chosen leaves us with numbers that are too difficult to deal with quickly and easily – which is one of the main advantages of doing estimations.

To estimate in a division sum round off to the nearest 10 or 100 (depending on the question and the size of the numbers involved), cross off and forget 0's which are common to both the number being divided and the divisor, then divide the remaining digits as usual

example $94 \div 27$

Round off the numbers to the nearest 10 $90 \div 30$
Cross off a 0 in each and forget them $9 \div 3 = 3$
Estimated answer is 3 (exact answer is 3, with a remainder of 3).

Example   722 ÷ 27

Round off to the nearest 10	720 ÷ 30
Cross off a 0 in each and forget them	72 ÷ 3

(This may be too difficult!) 72 ÷ 3 = 24
But you can start again with the estimate   722 ÷ 27
Round off the numbers   700 ÷ 30
(to nearest 100 and nearest 10 respectively)
70 ÷ 3 Cross off the 0 and put it in the answer   0
7 ÷ 3 (roughly)   2
Estimated answer is 20 (exact answer is 26 with 20 remainder)

Example   539 ÷ 87
Round off the numbers to the nearest 100   500 ÷ 100
5 ÷ 1 = Estimated answer is 5 (exact answer is 6 with 17 remainder)

Example   917 ÷ 128
Round off the numbers to the nearest 100   900 ÷ 100
Cross off 00 in each and forget about them   9 ÷ 1
9 ÷ 1 = 9
Estimated answer is 9 (exact answer is 7 with 21 remainder)

It is clear that the more complicated the sum is, the less near the estimate is likely to be; nevertheless it gives an idea of the size of the answer, which should show up any glaring errors in the calculations for an exact answer.

Later in this book students will be able to deal better with remainders by using decimals, and/or, by giving an answer correct to the number of significant figures asked for in the question (p. 106).

The division symbol

- Draw a circle and ask the student to put the division symbol in the centre.
- Colour the circle with a favourite colour.
- Discuss what the symbol represents. Talk about the sort of answers you would expect if you divide one number by another. Give several examples.
- Do an estimate and then use apparatus to find an accurate answer. Discuss that the number is always smaller than either number involved. (Of course, this is true only while we are using numbers greater than 1 in the divisor.)
- Ask what words the student would use to describe the symbol and then put those words around the symbol. If possible, make a wall chart with

the symbol plus the words he associates with that symbol so that it can be put on a wall for constant review.

- Try the following questions, and perhaps some more, to see if he can tell you what kind of calculation he would do to find a solution.
  Divide 10 by 5.
  How many 2's are there in 8?
  Share 15 between 5.

Symbol for division

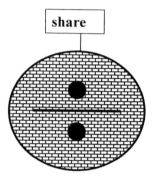

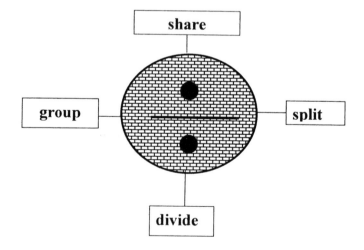

Single symbol for division

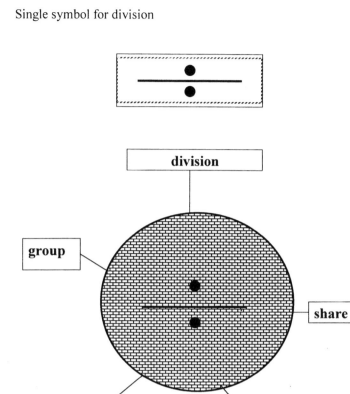

Examples of Division

Estimate, then calculate accurately
Use a table square, 1–100 square and/or a number line

(a)

10 ÷ 2,	8 ÷ 4,	10 ÷ 5	10 ÷ 1
24 ÷ 6	20 ÷ 5	32 ÷ 4	18 ÷ 3
70 ÷ 10	56 ÷ 8	64 ÷ 8	81 ÷ 9

Some of the following have remainders, show this as r followed by the number left over

(b)

2 | 46   4 | 84   3 | 93   5 | 55

(c)

2 | 83   5 | 58   7 | 78   4 | 86

(d)

3 | 75   6 | 84   8 | 96   2 | 78

(e)

5 | 76   7 | 94   3 | 57   4 | 61

(f)

6 | 546   3 | 126   3 | 141   5 | 445

(g)

7 | 721   6 | 606   8 | 817   3 | 108

(h)

16 | 32   18 | 54   14 | 70   13 | 91

(i)

21 | 58   32 | 72   44 | 98   15 | 79

(j)

16 | 192   33 | 396   17 | 376   18 | 960

Answers are on page 146

Chapter 8
Equals

$$=$$

This sign does not exactly mean that what is on one side is *the answer* to what is on the other. It means that the totals on each side are equal – the two sides balance.

As with a pair of scales, if we add the same number to both sides they will still balance

$6 - 4 = 2$ What happens if we add 4 to both sides?
$8 + 4 = 12$ What happens if we take away 4 from both sides?

On a calculator, pressing = will give you the answer to the sum just done.

63

Note for older students: This idea of balance gives you a basis for handling equations:

example   y − 7 = 2.

If we add 7 to both sides we can eliminate the number on the left without affecting the balance:

y − 7 + 7 = 2 + 7
y = 9

The equals symbol

- Draw a circle and ask the student to put the equals symbol in the centre.
- Colour the circle with a favourite colour.
- Discuss what the symbol represents. Write down a simple equation

example 2 + 3 = 5

Talk about what the equals sign means. (It is a balance between two sides. Use scales to show this in a practical way.)
- Ask what words he would use to describe the symbol and then put those words around the symbol. If possible make a wall chart with the symbol plus the words he associates with that symbol so that it can be put on a wall for constant review.
- Show a variety of ways that highlight the importance of the symbol and how it is vital in linking consecutive parts of calculations.

- example (a)   4 + 3 = 7

             (b)   6
                        +   2
                        ———————

                        ———————

             (c)   6 + 3 = 1 + 8

Students using calculators often press the equals sign wanting the answer to the problem they have just entered, not realizing that the sign represents a balance, because on a calculator the answer appears on the screen after the numbers entered have disappeared. Once they understand the concept of a balance they will be more aware of what they are doing, instead of just pressing keys. Later, when they are introduced to the term 'equation' they will recognize it as representing what they have been doing for years!

Symbol for equals

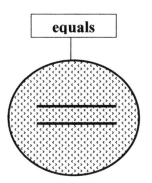

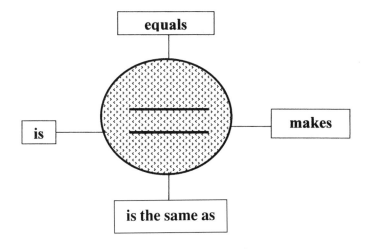

Single symbol for equals

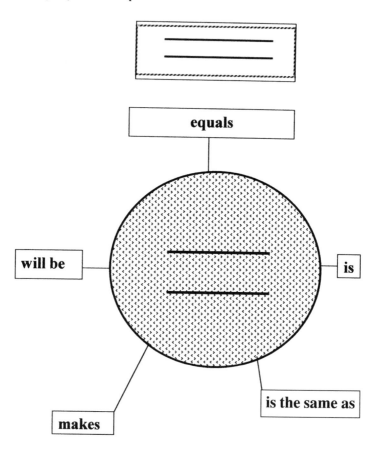

Chapter 9
Summary of the four operations

Addition is
      1. the piling up of separate items
  or 2. an advance up a scale.

    It can be done in either direction (commutative).

Subtraction is the inverse process to addition.
      1. It can mean taking away of separate items
  or 2. movement down a scale.
      3. Sometimes the process is used to find the
         difference between two numbers. It can
         not be done in either direction (non-commutative).

Multiplication is a quick way of doing a series of additions of the
    same number; instead of $3+3+3$, use 3×3.

The answer in both cases is the total, and you can work in either direction
in both addition and multiplication (commutative principle). This is useful
for multiplication tables, as e.g. 4×8 is the same as 8×4.

Division is a quick way of doing a series of subtractions of the
    same number down to 0.

You cannot work in either direction with either subtraction or division.
The answer in a division sum is *how many times* you remove a given
number to reach nought, and this will tell you how many people (or
groups) could have a share in it. Division is the inverse of multiplication.

Look at the five basic symbols (page 69) with students, and see if they can remember what they represent. Talk about the symbols with them, and if you write down the answers or tape them you will see how far they have got with their understanding. Depending on these, you can focus on any difficulties.

Look particularly at the + and × symbols and discuss that × is a quick way of doing addition.

Ask what is the relation between:

the two symbols on the left?
the two symbols on the right?
the top two symbols?
the bottom two symbols?

The Five Symbols

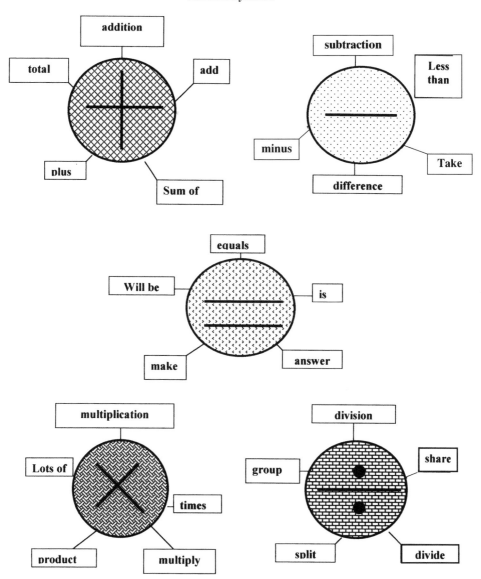

THE FOUR OPERATIONAL RULES

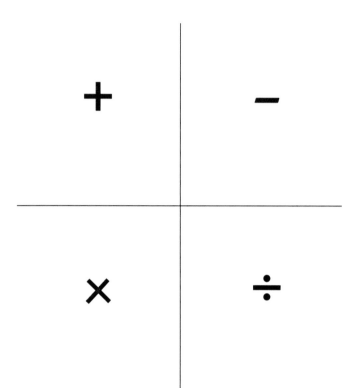

Chapter 10
Calculators

Now that calculators are an integral part of most mathematics courses, it is essential that all pupils are confident with the techniques of their use. Exercise books for practice are widely available.

Introducing the calculator

When a new calculator is purchased it will have a comprehensive manual to explain its functions, but this is often written in several different languages and is so technical that few students bother to read it. In our experience, most dyslexic students are unable to find the correct page written in the language that they understand, so that they never attempt to read any of the technical instructions or, if they do, they understand little of the meaning. It is a good idea, therefore, to make a *simple* manual, getting students to record, in words that they understand, instructions for particular functions that they will find useful. After a good introduction to using a calculator there needs to be careful discussion about the function of each key.

Type of calculator to choose

Clarity of display is an important element when choosing a calculator. Calculators need to be silent if group work is being done, with visual displays only; talking calculators are useful for individual lessons and homework and these can be either battery or solar operated. Students must be responsible for them and must make sure that they are in good working order. They can be encouraged to keep a spare battery as a standby. A student should have the same calculator that the teacher uses, and the one used by the majority of his peer group.

Benefits

Once a student has become proficient with his calculator he has a powerful tool at his disposal that will enable him to succeed. Since he can succeed, statements such as:

'I can't do tables'.
'I'm hopeless at subtraction'.
'Division is beyond me'.

are no longer valid, and the student can find success at a basic level. Consequently he will be more inclined to tackle more advanced material with a positive attitude when he no longer has the problem of working out a 'tables sum' in the middle of a calculation. He is more likely to concentrate and think a problem through to arrive at an accurate solution.

Becoming familiar with the calculator – basic function keys

The student needs to become familiar with each key that he will use, knowing not only its position, but also its name. It helps if students can be encouraged either to draw a calculator using colours and textures to show clearly +, ×, −, ÷, =, decimal point and zero and the position of these keys, or to make a 3D calculator display. Smooth card, rough sandpaper and fluorescent colours all add to the excitement of getting to know the calculator. Here is a simplified diagram.

7	8	9	C	AC
4	5	6	×	÷
1	2	3	+	−
0	●		=	M +

Students should be encouraged to press the keys *with their fingers* to check by touch that they have entered the correct number; they should be discouraged from using pencils or pens to press them, because they are more clumsy with these and many errors will result.

Reading the display on the calculator needs much practice, especially as it has to be read from left to right consistently, with place value, as usual, playing an important part in indicating the size of the number. If a student is experiencing difficulty over this, a large display panel can be made of cardboard, with loose numbers to be placed on it to make an extra-large display at the same time as the teacher puts the identical number on the calculator to allow him to compare the two. It is quite a good idea to start every lesson by allowing a student to read several numbers off the calculator to give him confidence.

Sequence is important, as keys have to be pressed in a strict order to obtain a correct answer, yet this is not necessarily the order of the English words. For instance 'Divide 36 by 9' can be put into the calculator in that order, but 9 divided by 36 has to be read from right to left first, so it is safer to transcribe before entering the number.

The equals sign also poses a few problems. If students have become used to pressing it quickly to obtain an answer to a sum, they do not readily associate it with the 'balancing' function it performs in an equation

e.g. $3 + 4 = 6 + 1$

They also need to understand that they need to press that key to conclude a function before proceeding with the next stage of the calculation even when there is no such sign in the written sum

e.g. $(6+4) - 7$

Press equals sign here

Here after the bracket has been worked out the equals sign key has to be pressed and again, of course, at the end.

Once again careful discussion beforehand can pre-empt any snags that may lead to errors in the use of the calculator.

Estimation

Estimation skills are very important in using the calculator. One needs to be sure that the answer is 'about the right size'. Dyslexic students are often loath to switch to an approximate number, e.g. 25 for 24.2, in order to have some idea of the size of the answer. They are not very adaptable, and feel that they have enough problems using the answer in the sum, without adding this pointless exercise! However once they realize how their performance is improved by this technique, which is a most important part of mathematics, they begin to see its advantages not only when using the calculator, but also in everyday life in the outside world. By incorporating estimation throughout lessons one can persuade students of its importance. We have found it useful to divide a page into two like this:

ESTIMATE   ACCURATE

A rough estimate can be recorded and then the calculator used to check. Students are really amused and delighted to see how near their estimated answer is to the one produced by the calculator. As they proceed they often acquire more advanced techniques of estimation and improve their understanding of the methods that they are using, and this provides a good foundation for more advanced investigations.

The decimal point

Another source of difficulty is the decimal point. Students:

        1. Don't see it.
or   2. Recognize it but ignore it.
or   3. Forget to put it in.
or   4. Know it is there, read the number correctly, but press the '0' key instead.

Displays with decimal points in them need much practice. Making large cardboard digits and a large plastic decimal point on a backing of velcro is extremely helpful.

e.g.
    Take the number   26.52

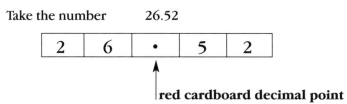

red cardboard decimal point

The student reads the number and himself puts the decimal point in the correct place. He reads the number again, enters it on the calculator and reads it again. This too is a valuable exercise to start a lesson.

Money sums

Problems to do with money can be solved using the calculator. However, students need to be told and shown not only that zero on the calculator is important, but also that the calculator often misses out the final zero of the written form after a decimal point, thus presenting students with further difficulties.

e.g. **60p is shown as .6 so 6p on a calculator is .06**

Much work needs to be done on this vital aspect of money sums on the calculator, for even students working at advanced levels sometimes read off an incorrect amount and turn an otherwise excellent piece of work into one that is flawed. Practice with the routine of the calculator really does make perfect.

Fractions

The fraction key is an important one for a dyslexic student, since the cry 'I can't do tables' is usually followed by 'I can't understand fractions'. The fraction key (abbreviated to FK below) says

$$a \, ^b/_c$$

Students can use this to work out calculations involving fractions once they understand how it works.

To put ½ on the calculator:
                                                    Calculator display

Press 1   1
Press FK   1 ⌋
Press 2   1 ⌋ 2

1 ⌋ 2 is ½ on the calculator

To put 1 ½ on the calculator:
                                                    Calculator display

Press 1   >   1
Press FK   1 ⌋
Press 1   >   1 ⌋ 1
Press FK   1 ⌋ 1 ⌋
Press 2   >   1 ⌋ 1 ⌋ 2

1 ⌋ 1 ⌋ 2 is 1 ½ on the calculator

To complete the simple calculation ½ + 1 ½ all the above instructions are followed, with the insertion of the + sign in between, and the = sign at the end. A correct answer will then be displayed.

Converting a vulgar fraction to a decimal fraction

Another function of the key is turning a vulgar fraction into a decimal fraction.

> e.g. ½ is displayed 1 ⌐ 2 on the calculator
> Press =
> Press FK
> It will then be displayed as a decimal fraction.
> (Press FK again and it will revert to the vulgar fraction.)

Negative numbers

Negative numbers can be entered into a calculator by using the key +/−. To put −3 on the calculator press 3, then +/- and the display will show −3.

In all these uses of the calculator, procedures and sequence are very important if the correct answer is to be obtained. Each key must be discussed carefully and practised until the student feels entirely confident with it.

The memory key M+

The memory key M+ is useful also, but students always need to be aware that it needs to be cancelled. They need to press **CM** or **MC** to clear memory. Students with language difficulties need to recognize the abbreviation and be confident over the use of the memory key.

Once the basic function keys have been mastered, other keys can be explored and gradually introduced into calculations. It is necessary to discuss at all times the purpose of the key, its function and how it can help in the solution of the problem. The procedures can be recorded in the student's own manual so that he will always have them for easy reference. Much practice is always required to make the student confident with his calculator and able to use it easily and competently to achieve success.

Students throughout should be encouraged to *write down* methods they are about to follow which incorporate the use of the calculator. This is not an easy task, as many students would prefer to record nothing, just use the calculator and write down an answer! If their calculations are correct, with all procedures entered and carried out competently, the answer will be acceptable. On the other hand, if they have recorded nothing and become confused part way through, then they have to go back to the beginning each time, as they have nothing to which they can refer. Should they do this several times, they become frustrated, and in all probability will give up. Therefore, if good habits can be instilled at the start success is more likely to be achieved.

In SATS and other examinations students are told not to use a calculator by a sign showing a calculator crossed out, something like this:

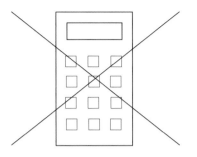

Students need to have it explained to them that this means that they may not use a calculator *for that particular question only* and does not apply to the whole paper.

Note

We have not mentioned a number of keys that appear on calculators, because for basic purposes a dyslexic student does not need to use them.

Chapter 11
Money

Dyslexic students who struggle with estimation are bound to have difficulty with money and shopping. They are unable to work out how much money they need to pay for goods, or how much change they should receive. A dyslexic student can, like the rest of us, pay by credit card or offer notes, relying on the cashier to work out the total and give the correct change. However, most of us can estimate and double-check on the bill, and be in a position, if necessary, to query the total, should it be vastly different from the expected one. It is important for dyslexic students to be able to do this.

Recording of money

Dyslexic students obviously recognize that e.g. £3.65 is a price. They should realize, first of all, that our monetary system has a decimal basis, and is recorded like that, with the £ sign for the pounds, then a decimal point, or sometimes a colon, and the pence recorded as hundredths of a £1. So £3.65 is £3 and 65 pence. One hundred pence will of course be recorded as a pound. They will need plenty of practice reading off sums in written form. Although the £ sign comes before the number, we read it as three pounds. 'p' does not figure in the written form, except sometimes at the top of a number of prices on a total bill, e.g.

£	p
3	65
5	27

etc.

They will also need to recognize the wording used to express the amount in ordinary words, and the abbreviations used, e.g. 'Three pounds sixty-five'.

Coinage

When it comes to the coins and notes in their purses, there is, of course, a coin for £1, and a coin for 10p (.1 of a pound, the first column after the decimal point), and for 1p, (.01 of a pound, the second column after the decimal point). However for convenience there are also some extra coins and notes – 2p, 5p, 20p, 50p and £2 coins, and £5 (500p) £10 (1,000p), £20 (2,000p), and indeed £50 (5,000p) notes, although students may not meet the last of these very often! Only the £10 will have a representation in the decimal system. Students will need to handle the coins and become familiar with them, their size and feel and the metal they are made of and how they can be exchanged for other coins. It is best to show them real coins at first, to make the link with real life; later imitation ones will do. To help blind people, the £1 coins are much thicker, and 50p coins have seven sides (why not five?!) and so have the much smaller 20p coins. It is not necessarily the case that the larger coins are worth more. (See illustrations, page 139).

Handling money transactions

When students are asking for change, they will probably find it easier to 'add on' from the sum owing to the amount of money they have given to calculate the change required. Thus if he spends 4p and gives a 10p coin, he should start with the 4p and count from there up to the 10p (i.e. 6). (He must *not*, of course, count *both* the 4p *and* the 10p.) If he started to count backwards he would probably get confused. If he is not doing a written calculation his strategy need not be the same as everyone else's; it is more important that he understands it, is confident and gets the right answer. If later he is doing mental tests and is asked how he did it, it will not matter if his method is different from that of everybody else in the group. Developing efficient, quick mental arithmetic strategies is an important part of his mathematical education.

Money lines

Students can make a money line initially up to 10p, and be asked to place coins on this. Later they can use a £1.00 money line, putting various amounts on it. It is possible to make horizontal calculations using a money line, just as with numbers without the £ sign.

Checklist

Does the student:
* know the money words and abbreviations?
  Pence = p; Pound = £1
* understand the expressions 'how much?' 'how many?' 'owe' 'change' 'expensive (dear)' 'too much' 'too little'
* recognize the coins 1p, 2p, 5p, 10p, 20p, 50p, £1.00, £2.00 from their looks and feel?

Can he:
* count money (How much have you got?)
* give change from 10p, 20p, 50p, £1.00? (Can he say how he worked it out?)
* give the correct money for goods he wishes to buy?
* give more money than he owes and work out how much change he should receive? (Can he say how he worked it out?)

Written calculations

When students have become sure of these skills, so that they can confidently add strings of single-digit numbers, then a single-digit with a two-digit number, and eventually two two-digit numbers, they will move on to doing written money calculations, recording money using a decimal notation for money, with a point dividing the pounds from the pence. They must understand the connection between tenths and hundredths of a decimal number and the pence columns.

Teachers should check that students understand the words in a written money problem, and can talk about the methods to use and the appropriate procedures to use before beginning to record. It should be left to the student at this stage whether he records horizontally, using his number line practice, or vertically.

When their skills become automatic and they begin to speed up, then, of course, they must be shown how to record money accurately – as with sums involving decimals they must be careful that the dots line up, so that the numbers are in their correct columns.

They may need practice in writing the £ sign clearly, as some find this quite difficult.

Helpful strategies

* Students like to make 'postage stamps' with values 1p, 2p, 5p, 10p,

20p, 50p and £1.00 and use real coins to link with the stamps. Then they can be given 'envelopes' to post, putting the correct value for postage told to them.
e.g. 'This letter needs stamps to the value of 27p.'
- Situations of written problems can be worked out practically too.
e.g. 'I have 24p which I want to divide equally between 4 children. How much will each child receive?'
'I have 24 p and I want to give 6p to as many children as possible. How many children will receive 6p?' (This can be solved by doing repeated subtraction and linking that to division, see page 57.)

We have included 'Percentages with money' and 'Fractions with money' here, but the teacher may need to come back to these after completing the relevant chapters (16 and 13 respectively).

Percentages with money

If students have dealt with simple percentages they can then apply the concept to money. It is possible to use a number line for this, so that they can see easily that 50% is 50p, 25% is 25p etc.

If easy numbers are used, students can work out:

50% of	£10.00	£20.00	£36.00	£40.00
25% of	£10.00	£60.00	£100.00	£200.00
10% of	£10.00	£20.00	£50.00	£100.00

They can use a few percentages as a basis for working out more complex ones by doubling, halving etc.

e.g. (1)   Find 15% of £60.00:

10% of £60.00	=	£6.00
5% of £60.00 (half of above)	=	£3.00
ADD the two together		
15% of £60.00 (£6.00 + £3.00)	=	£9.00

(2)   Find 17½ % of £60.00

10% of £60.00	=	£ 6.00
5% of £60.00	=	£ 3.00
2½ % of £60.00 (half the above)	=	£ 1.50
17½ % of £60.00 (£6.00 + £3.00 + £1.50)	=	£10.50

If students acquire the habit of constantly estimating before working out answers, they will soon see connections between past and new skills, and realize that money problems are merely variations of procedures that they have used before.

Fractions and money

A £1.00 number line can be used to show fractions of £1.00.

Half of £1.00 is 50p.
A quarter is 25p.
Three-quarters is 75p.
One tenth is 10p.
One fifth is 20p.

(Decimal notation can be linked to this when decimals have been studied so that a table can be made, which students can carry around with them to reinforce these facts.)

$£^1/_2$	=	£0.50	=	50p
$£^1/_4$	=	£0.25	=	25p
$£^3/_4$	=	£0.75	=	75p
$£^1/_{10}$	=	£0.10	=	10p
$£^1/_5$	=	£0.20	=	20p

Later on, when students are confident with these basic fractions, they can do more complex calculations, e.g.

$^1/_2$ of £5.00, $^1/_2$ of £6.00, $^3/_4$ of £10, $^1/_{10}$ of £20, $^1/_5$ of £50.00.

Throughout it is important to do estimations of the answers, followed by correct calculations, then check on the calculator. Such procedures will enable students to improve their skills in all these areas.

Discussing these procedures on a calculator will enable the students to make the link between the word 'of' and the multiplication symbol. In working out 1/2 of £26.30, the student will realize that he needs to divide £26.30 by 2, but on a calculator he has a choice:

He can either enter

	26.30	divide by	2
or	26.30	multiplied by	$\frac{1}{2}$ or 0.5

and he will get the same answer.

The flexibility allows different approaches to be used.

Chapter 12
Time

Telling the time, estimating and understanding the passage of time, remembering the day/week/month, and in association with this remembering what he or she should be doing at that specific time, all cause very great problems for dyslexics.

Learning to tell the time from both an analogue and a digital clock requires many skills, so having the opportunity to work through all the small steps to acquire these skills is very important. There are also students who do not require this step-by-step approach, but do need to get accustomed to viewing a clock from various different angles and judging the time, particularly with an analogue clock; they have to realize the importance of the exact position of the hands. For a digital clock they have to be careful about left and right so that they begin to read in the correct place, and the function of the dots needs to be discussed – often an anxious student will not even notice them.

Vocabulary associated with time

* Days of the week, day, night, morning, afternoon, evening, today, tomorrow.
* Abbreviations:

    Monday – Mon. Tuesday – Tues. Wednesday – Wed.
    Thursday – Thurs. Friday – Fri. Saturday – Sat.
    Sunday – Sun.
    minutes – mins. seconds – secs. hours – hrs.
* Seasons   colder, hotter   Spring, Summer, Autumn, Winter.
* Clock   face, hands
                o'clock, half past, quarter past (quarter to)

The analogue clock (work sheet p. 140)

Make a clock with just one long hand in a special colour – discuss position.

Make a clock with just one short hand in a special colour – discuss position.

Put in the numbers 1–12. (Play a game to see if students can do this with eyes shut.)

Count in fives so that the numbers are correctly placed.

Make use of both hands to see what happens when they both move, emphasizing that the long hand points to the minutes and the short finger points to the hours.

Look at hour times – 1 o'clock, 2 o'clock, etc., moving the hands to the correct times when doing this.

Discuss 'half past' by colouring half the clock in a different colour, then 'quarter past'.

Then use a clock which records both minutes and hours, with the number 1 having 5 written near it, etc., but do this only when the students are confident with the earlier stages.

You may decide to read past times only, so that you will read '45 minutes past 1', etc.

The digital clock

Students are often much happier reading this, because they can relate to their video machines, computers, audio players, all of which show digital time.

However, they need to make the connection between digital and analogue time, so will need to read both, using the same words to link the two. Thus if they see 1.05, they will read it as 'five minutes past one'. They will also need to practise the reverse process, reading the analogue clock as 'twenty minutes past two', but writing it as 2.20.

Eventually using an analogue clock with a digital display helps to connect the two.

a.m and p.m.

- Teachers need to discuss that a.m. is before lunch-time (i.e. 12 o'clock mid-day) and p.m. is afternoon (after 12 mid-day until midnight).
- The connection has to be made with the 24 hour clock. Times recorded as more than 12 are p.m. times.
- The 24 hour clock always has 4 digits when written. So it has to be pointed out that times up to and including nine fifty-nine a.m. must always begin with a 0, e.g. 09.59

- Conversion of 24 hour time to 12 hour time and vice versa. Students find it easier to add/subtract a 2, then a 10, as shown in the following examples:

  (1) To change 6,55 p.m. to 24 hour time
       Add 12 to the first number only
       6.55 p.m.   +2   =   8.55   +10   =   18.55

  (2) To change 22.25 from 24 hour time to 12 hour time
       Subtract 12 from the first number only
       22.25   −2   =   20.25   −10   =   10.25 p.m.

Some students are able to do this easily, but others need to develop a procedure for recognizing the time as a p.m. time (12 hour clock) and then how to do the addition calculation to end up with the correct 24 hour clock time, and likewise the reverse process.

The calendar

Students need to relate this to time in their own lives, making a timetable for their whole day, then making one for their time in school.

- They need to know the months in the year with the number of days in each, so that as they progress through school these important numbers are constantly in their minds.
- Knuckle patterns help with this – long months are on the knuckles, short months in the dips between. February's particularly short number and variability has to be stressed.
- They need to practise writing out the days and months of the year to help their spelling, as these words can cause difficulties. Recognizing

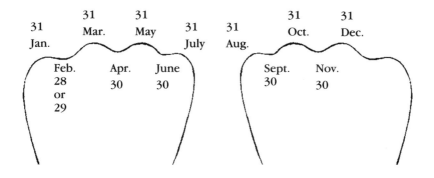

their own and other students' birthdays often helps. It is useful to practise asking what month/day comes before/after this one.
- They need practice in reading a calendar. This enables them to spot easily where a new week begins, etc., so that in time they will be able to work out questions such as 'What will the date be 3 weeks from the 3rd of April?'
- They have to learn the use of abbreviations 'st' 'nd' 'rd' 'th' in dates.

Drawing pictures and putting in events in their own lives, and the seasons when they happen, makes the calendar real to them. Some like to imagine the year as a circle; other prefer a sort of horseshoe shape.

Passage of time

- Estimating a minute more or less accurately may help with this difficult skill.
- Remembering what day it is can be helped by linking it with a specific happening that is meaningful to the student.
- Students who travel a good deal by rail can often relate to how much time they've spent in the train when travelling, e.g. from London to Edinburgh, and note the time when they arrive.

School timetables

Students have to cope with timetables from the first moment they arrive in secondary school. At first they are guided by their teacher and other adults, who tell them what to do and where to go at specific times. Later they have to begin to take responsibility for themselves, so they need to understand school timetables. Dyslexic students often have difficulty reading these; as they struggle to read the subject words, they often do not notice the days or the times referred to in the table.

Teachers and others need to talk a student through an individual timetable. It is important to pick out a particular lesson that he really enjoys on each day of the week, which will remind him what day it is. If these subjects are highlighted with special colours, in time he will begin to connect each of those subjects with other events that occur before and after it. In this way he will learn what equipment and what books he needs for the day.

A student needs to have several copies of his individual timetable available, so that losing one will not necessarily mean disaster. Teachers should have clear, easy-to-read timetables on view to help them. Daily, weekly, monthly and yearly timetables should be readily available and discussed, so that they are understood by all students. All too often they are set out in such a complex way that even some adults would struggle to make sense of them.

Bus and train timetables

Bus and train timetables use the 24 hour clock system, so students will need to refer to their own digital watches to interpret them; they need specific lessons on such timetables, as they are quite complicated – first how a journey is recorded on a timetable in a column and that the times given are for the stations where the train or bus will stop, next how they can work out the length of time taken for a journey by subtracting the start time from the arrival time. If a student is using a particular bus route regularly he can be shown how to find his particular bus in the timetable, perhaps colouring it in. In theory he needs to be able to look up what time the next bus will arrive should he miss the first one, but buses are not necessarily on time!

Chapter 13
Fractions

This chapter is concerned with what fractions *are* and how they are recorded mathematically. Addition, subtraction, multiplication and division of fractions come in a later chapter.

Fractions are **equal** parts, bits or pieces of a whole. Much practice needs to be done dividing different things into such parts, as illustrated by the pages on fractions in the Appendix, and then putting them together again to see how they form the whole. This last part should not be omitted as the converse is not always as obvious to dyslexics as it may seem to the teacher. It is important that many different shapes and other examples be used so that pupils are not tied to one, but can generalize to the concept of a fraction as being a part in relation to a whole *of any kind*

A fraction is recorded as two numbers because it expresses the **relation** of the number of pieces to the whole. The *bottom* number (the 'denominator') gives the number of equal pieces into which the whole is divided, while the *top* number (the 'numerator') gives the number of those pieces that we have here and now. It is important that pupils fully understand this.

e.g. $\dfrac{1}{4}$ means that the whole consists of 4 parts, of which we have 1 here – and if we add 4 of them together we shall get one whole.

It is useful, although not absolutely essential, for the pupil to know the terms 'denominator' and 'numerator'. The pupil might find it helpful to remember which is which by noting that the longer word (5 syllables as against 4) refers to the bottom number, in the same way as the bigger number is usually the bottom number in a fraction.

$$\frac{\text{nu/mer/a/tor}}{\text{de/nom/in/a/tor}}$$

Improper fractions

If there are more pieces than will make the whole it can be written like this:

e.g. $\dfrac{9}{4}$

This is called an 'improper fraction'. Why 'improper'? Well presumably because the 'proper' function of fractions is to say what part the top is of one whole, and there are too many parts on top for that. Consequently at the end of a sum it is considered more 'proper' to rearrange an 'improper fraction' as a whole or wholes plus any remaining fractions. **The pupil must be taught to do this**.

e.g. $\dfrac{9}{4}$ = $2\,{}^{1}/_{4}$

(One must be careful, however, not to do this with a ratio. A ratio *can* be written like a fraction but would no longer be a ratio if it were changed to a whole plus a fraction. It is best to teach your pupil always to write a ratio like this 5:4, to avoid confusion, and not to tell him of any other way.)

Equivalent fractions

It can easily be demonstrated by dividing up a block or a circle that a half is 'the same as' or equivalent to two quarters or four eighths. The **relationship** between the two numbers, which is what a fraction is expressing, stays the same if you multiply **both** by the same number. This is useful if one wants to add two fractions together and they have different denominators – you can alter one to fit with the other,

e.g. $\dfrac{1}{12}$ + $\dfrac{3}{4}$

Multiply the right-hand fraction by 3 (top and bottom!) and that will give it a denominator of 12 too. Then the numerator can be added to the left-hand one. Two fractions of different denominators cannot be added, because the 'pieces' into which the whole is divided are not the same.

Equivalent fractions are also useful when simplifying a number. **The pupil must always do this in presenting his answer whenever it is possible**.

Thus an answer cannot be: $\dfrac{6}{12}$ it must be simplified to $\dfrac{1}{2}$

by dividing **both** top and bottom by six.

Getting accustomed to fractions

Plenty of practice is needed in counting in fractions and in 'reading' situations in terms of fractions, whether from pictorial representations or in maths problems expressed in ordinary language and recording them in the right symbols, and likewise the converse.

Pupils also need practice in understanding how fractions have to be treated differently from whole numbers. Both numbers have to be involved in any operation, not just one, and when two fractions are multiplied together the answer is smaller not bigger! (A half 'of' a quarter is an eighth.) Note that 'of' in this context equals 'times' in mathematical notation. Giving various examples like this, or illustrating it pictorially, e.g. in a square or a circle will be needed to convince them of this important difference between fractions and whole numbers. There are examples in the Appendix.

Sums with fractions

1. ADDITION AND SUBTRACTION

Adjustment of the denominator

The **bottom** number (the denominator) tells you what pieces – what units – you are using. If these are different for two fractions it is not possible to add them together or subtract one from another. The units have to be the same.

If you were asked to add 4 exercise books to 200 pages of paper and say 'how many', you would ask 'How many **what**?!' Only by counting the pages in the exercise books, say 50 pages each, could you give an answer in terms of **pages**. The units of the first item have to be changed from 'books' to 'pages' to match the second item.

50 *pages* × 4 = 200 *pages* – plus the other 200 pages = 400 *pages*

Similarly, if you want to add two fractions that have different denominators you **FIRST** have to put them into the same denominations or units.

$$\frac{1}{2} \;+\; \frac{3}{4} \;=\; \frac{2}{4} \;+\; \frac{3}{4} \;=\; \frac{5}{4} \;=\; 1\,{}^{1}\!/_{4}$$

Multiplying the denominator and numerator of the first fraction by 2 (to make the denominator 4 like that in the second fraction) gives an 'equivalent fraction' (see previous section) and the fraction is still the same size overall.

Then the addition is possible. The same process is necessary before you do subtractions.

To *add and subtract fractions*

Having adjusted the two fractions as above when necessary you then **add the two numerators only** or **subtract one numerator from the other** as the case may be. In the above example we added *two* quarters and *three* quarters. The denominators must not be added, as that would change the units we are working in – quarters.

Sometimes the adjustment of the denominator is not quite so easy, e.g.

$$\frac{3}{5} \;+\; \frac{4}{7}$$

Since neither number can be expressed in the units of the other, *both denominators* have to be changed – into some unit that both 5 and 7 will 'go into'. That number is 35.

To turn fifths into thirty-fifths, we multiply top and bottom by 7. To turn sevenths into thirty-fifths, we multiply top and bottom by 5. Now they are both in the same units and we can add them.

$$\frac{21}{35} \;+\; \frac{20}{35} \;=\; \frac{41}{35} \;=\; 1\,{}^{6}\!/_{35}$$

The number 35 was found by multiplying the two numbers 5 and 7 together. That *must* be a number that both will go into. In some cases multiplying the denominators will give a bigger number than is necessary, but you can always simplify at the end, e.g.

$$\frac{3}{10} \;+\; \frac{5}{12} \;=\; \frac{36}{120} \;+\; \frac{50}{120} \;=\; \frac{86}{120} \;=\; \frac{43}{60}$$

Of course, if you can spot earlier that 60 will do from the beginning, because both 10 and 12 will 'go into' 60, so much the better!

Do not go on to multiplication and division of fractions until pupils are totally at home with the above, and then impress on them that they must not use the above procedures for multiplication and division, which are quite different.

2. MULTIPLICATION

It is important to realize that in multiplying fractions the answer will be smaller, not larger. Why? because in multiplying e.g. a half by two-thirds you are asking for half of that two-thirds, which must be less than the two-thirds you started with. This may take several demonstrations with material for the pupil to understand, and we have put some diagrams in the Appendix to help. The mathematical procedure is quite simple; the numerators are multiplied together and the two denominators are multiplied together, e.g.

$$\frac{1}{2} \times \frac{2}{3} = \frac{2}{6}$$

That this *is* the right answer can easily be demonstrated by dividing a whole circle or block into both thirds and ninths. A two-thirds piece will be found to be six ninths, and two-thirds of *that piece* is four ninths.

3. DIVISION

Note that this time you are going to expect a *higher* number! (e.g. How many times does a half go into one? Answer – 'two times'.)

From the above one would expect that dividing fractions would involve dividing numerator by numerator and denominator by denominator, and indeed that is fine as long as *both* the numerator will 'go into' the numerator *and* the denominator will 'go into' the denominator, e.g.

$$\frac{9}{16} \div \frac{3}{8} = \frac{3}{2} = 1\frac{1}{2}$$

Usually, of course, this is not the case. So you have to use a trick. Remember that the dividing line in a fraction is a way of expressing division. So if we reverse the fraction, we are reversing the division (multiplying). Then if we reverse the *process* used (multiply instead of dividing) the result should be equivalent to what we started with – we have done a **double reversal.** This is like saying 'I shall NOT NOT go to town today.' i.e. 'I shall go'!

e.g.

$$\frac{3}{7} \div \frac{5}{9} = \frac{3}{7} \times \frac{9}{5} = \frac{27}{35}$$

So what you do with division of fractions is **turn the second fraction upside down and multiply**.

Chapter 14
Decimals

The word 'decimal' is short for 'decimal fraction'. Decimals are indeed fractions; they are fractions which are reckoned in tenths, e.g. one tenth, seven hundredths, three thousandths, etc.

These can of course be written as fractions in the usual way

e.g. $\dfrac{1}{10}$ $\dfrac{7}{100}$ $\dfrac{3}{1,000}$

However, because we have a Base Ten Number System (see pp. 24–25), this system can be extended to include numbers less than one which are divisible by ten, and then such numbers can be written much more simply, observing the usual rules for Place Value. The point on the scale where whole numbers finish and decimals begin is marked by a decimal point. Numbers in each column represent one-tenth of those in the column before as one moves from left to right.

It will be useful to set this out in a diagram, with a large and prominent decimal point made of plastic or plasticine in a bright colour and plastic numbers. The fractions given above have been inserted as examples.

TH	H	T	U	•	Tenths	Hundredths	Thousandths
			0	•	1		
			0	•	0	7	
			0	•	0	0	3

The numbers can be moved to the next left column to multiply by ten, two columns along to multiply by a hundred, etc. and the new number read off. The columns can be colour-coded.

97

Multiplying the above numbers by ten will give the following:

$$1.0 \qquad 0.7 \qquad 0.03$$

Moving the original numbers to the right is to divide by ten, a hundred, etc. Dividing the original decimals by ten will give these numbers:

$$0.01 \qquad 0.007 \qquad 0.0003$$

There should be plenty of practice of this. More complicated numbers should be used too, and the numbers read off

$$\text{e.g. } 26.3 \times 10 \qquad 4.85 \times 100 \quad \text{etc.}$$

Plenty of practice is needed reading such numbers, with the decimal point prominently displayed.

Putting a 0 if there are no units is good practice, e.g. 0.75, and 0's can always be added after the decimal point when there is no number in that column; this makes a sum clearer when adding a number which uses those decimal places, e.g.

$$\begin{array}{r} 2.000 \\ + 3.475 \end{array}$$

Reading decimals

Pupils will need plenty of practice in reading different numbers containing decimals to make sure that they have the place value correct. Practice with flash cards is also useful; the whole number can be highlighted in a prominent colour and the decimal point made really big.

Writing decimals

Using squared paper will emphasize the columns; the decimal point must be put on the line between whole numbers and tenths, but it can be highlighted. The decimal points have to be lined up one below the other on the same vertical line, and on the left of the decimal numbers.

It is always good practice to put in a 0 in the whole number column if there is no figure to enter there but a decimal follows after the decimal point.

Calculators

When inserting decimal numbers on a calculator it is a good precaution to read them aloud both before and after insertion to check for accuracy.

Fractions/decimals

The decimal equivalents of commonly used fractions should be made secure

$$\frac{1}{2} = 0.5 \qquad \frac{1}{4} = 0.25 \qquad \frac{3}{4} = 0.75$$

The equivalent percentages should also be taught at the appropriate age.

50%   25%   75%

It gives a better understanding of the meaning of decimal numbers if pupils practise turning decimals into fractions, and fractions – provided the denominator is divisible by ten – into decimals.

Sums with decimals

ADDITION AND SUBTRACTION OF DECIMALS

There is no particular difficulty with these once it is understood that the decimal system is an extension of the base ten system used for whole numbers. The place-value columns have to be strictly observed; **the decimal points must be lined up very carefully at the beginning, because the decimal point marks the place where we shift from a whole number column to a column for fractions of whole numbers.**

Thus 3.456 + 0.12 is written down as

$$3.40$$
$$+ 0.12$$

and 3.45 – 0.6 is written down as

$$3.45$$
$$- 0.60$$

MULTIPLICATION OF DECIMALS

This is quite simple when a number with a decimal in it is being multiplied by a whole number with no decimal, provided the decimal point is kept firmly in place

e.g.
$$\begin{array}{r} 4.64 \\ \times 3 \\ \hline 13.92 \end{array}$$

But when both numbers have a decimal in them it is a little more complicated.

When fractions are multiplied the result is a fraction of *smaller* value, as was pointed out on page 95. Similarly, when the decimal part of one number comes to be multiplied by the decimal part of the other number, the result will be a *smaller* decimal number, so there will be *more* decimal places in the answer.

With fractions, e.g.

$$\frac{12}{100} \times \frac{31}{100} = \frac{12 \times 31}{100 \times 100} = \frac{372}{10,000}$$

– the answer is in ten-thousandths, with more noughts than either of the originals, in fact **the number of noughts is that of the original denominators added together**.

Therefore, if we do it in decimal notation the answer will get into the ten-thousandths column (the fourth column from the decimal point), and **there will be as many decimal places as the originals had, added together.**

.12 × .31 has four decimal places altogether

and therefore the answer is going extend to four decimal places.

The sum is done as follows:

$$\begin{array}{r} 12 \\ \times 31 \\ \hline 12 \\ 360 \\ \hline 372 \end{array}$$

as if they were whole numbers, carefully preserving the columns, then put in the four decimal places, and the answer is:

.0372

This can be checked on the calculator. But see note at the end of this chapter

DIVISION OF DECIMALS

.36 ÷ .12

If we put it in the fraction notation, and then turn one fraction upside down and multiply (see Sums with Fractions section, page 95) we get

$$\frac{36}{100} \times \frac{100}{12}$$

The 100s cancel out and we are left with 36 ÷ 12. We can see that .36 ÷ .12 is the same as 36 ÷ 12. So we can do a decimal sum with whole numbers instead, by first multiplying both numbers by 100. As a matter of fact all that is necessary is to make the *divisor* a whole number (although of course *both* numbers must be multiplied).

$$\text{e.g. } 4.75 \div 0.5 \times 10 = 47.5 \div 5$$

With a more complicated number as divisor this might still involve a long division sum and might have to be done on the calculator, but it will be possible to estimate what sort of answer to expect.

$$\text{e.g. } 4.75 \div 0.25 \times 100 = 475 \div 25$$

There are four 25's in a hundred, 16 in 400, 20 in 500, so the answer will be something between 16 and 20. Actually the exact answer is 19, since 475 is just 25 less than 500.

Note

In multiplication of decimals there will be one or two occasions when adding the decimal places does not seem to work:

$$\text{e.g. } 0.5 \times 0.8 = 0.4\underline{0}$$

The final 0 counts as one of the two places, but is then discarded, and it does not appear on the calculator at all.

Chapter 15
Changing Fractions into Decimals/Correction to significant figures

1. Changing fractions into decimals.

Practical Strategies

Students can use number lines to make connections between fractions and decimals. Once they are familiar with a number line 1 to 10 they can begin to talk about a half and mark it on the line. Quarters and three-quarters can be gradually introduced. If the number line is on the floor, several students can be given both numbers and fractions and they can walk to stand in the correct spot. Once they are familiar with halves and

---

Prerequisite Skills

(1) Students must be able to read fractions

   i.e. $^1/_2$ says one half

   $^1/_4$ says one quarter

   $^3/_4$ says three quarters

(2) Students must understand that

1 is the same as	1.0	as well as	1.00	or	1.00000
2 =	2.0	=	2.00		
3 =	3.0	=	3.00		

because if they do not know this they will wonder just where you have found or conjured up the additional noughts when trying to divide 1 by 5.

(3) Students need to be familiar with the words

   'numerator' (the number on top of the dividing line)

   'denominator' (the number underneath the dividing line)

Mnemonic: denominator is a larger word with more syllables and therefore goes underneath, as the larger number in fractions usually does.

---

quarters, tenths can be shown and marked. Common decimal fractions such as 0.25, 0.5 and 0.75 can be introduced.

Strategies

• Look at the shape of a fraction and discuss the fact that the

e.g. $\dfrac{1}{4}$ $\dfrac{numerator}{denominator}$

The dots over and below the dividing line in the division symbol represent this shape.

$$\div$$

• Look at the fraction shape and imagine that the words 'divided by' are written on the dividing line.

$$\dfrac{numerator}{\boxed{divided\ by}}{denominator}$$

To change a fraction into a decimal

After looking at the fraction shape and imagining the words 'divided by', follow those instructions and divide the top number by the bottom number e.g.

      change $^1/_2$ to a decimal
      divide ($\div$) 1 by 2

$$
2\ \overline{\big|\ \begin{array}{ccccc} 0 & \bullet & 5 \\ 1 & \bullet & 0 \end{array}}
$$

Answer = 0.5

Changing Decimals into Fractions

To change a decimal into a fraction

• Draw the dividing line and put the digit 1 underneath (1 is the 1st digit) because the resulting fraction will be either

      $\dfrac{?}{10}$ or $\dfrac{?}{100}$ or $\dfrac{?}{1000}$

• Look at the decimal and count the number of digits after the decimal point

- Under the dividing line put the same number of noughts next to the 1 as there are digits after the decimal point
- Put the decimal number above the dividing line

e.g. (a)
   Change 0.3 into a fraction

- Draw the dividing line and put a 1 underneath

$$\frac{}{1}$$

- Look at the decimal and count the number of digits after the decimal point
- Under the dividing line put the same number of noughts next to the 1 as there are digits after the decimal point

- Put the decimal number above the dividing line

$$\frac{3}{1\quad0}$$

The answer is three tenths

e.g. (b)
   Change 0.14 into a fraction

- Draw the dividing line and put a 1 underneath

$$\frac{}{1}$$

- Look at the decimal and count the number of digits after the decimal point
- Under the dividing line put the same number of noughts next to the 1 as there are digits after the decimal point

$$\frac{}{1\quad0\quad0}$$

Put the decimal number above the dividing line

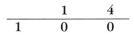

The answer is fourteen hundredths

This fraction can be simplified or cancelled down by dividing both top and bottom by 2

The answer would then be seven fiftieths

Cancelling Fractions

Dyslexic pupils would prefer not to cancel down as they have trouble remembering the sequence of the procedure. They may divide the top by 2 but they may forget to divide the bottom number and leave their answer as seven hundredths which is worse than not doing any cancelling. If they are able to use a calculator with a fraction key they can:

* enter the numerator, press the fraction key, enter the denominator
* press the equals key
* press the fraction key again
* and the fraction will be automatically reduced to its lowest terms.

2. Correction to significant figures

One is sometimes asked to give an answer corrected to a specific number of significant figures (SF or Sig. Fig.). Count from the left.

Noughts at the beginning of a number are not significant
    e.g. in .003 the first significant number is 3.
Noughts within the number *are* significant
    e.g. in 702.04 *both* noughts are significant.

Whether the number includes decimals is irrelevant to whether the numbers are significant.

The corrected number must be of the same *order* as the original – i.e.
    109 corrected to one significant figure is 100 not 1 or 10!
If the number *immediately after* the significant figure mentioned is 5 or more, the significant figure must be raised by 1.

Examples

1. Correct 862 to 1 significant figure.
    Put in a cut-off line after one digit – 8/62
    Look at the number after the line. More than 5? Yes. Add 1 to the 8.
    Add two 00's to keep the number in the same order of magnitude
    (i.e. in the hundreds).
    Answer 900.
2. Correct 32.5 to 1 significant figure.
    Put in the cut-off line – 3/2.8
    Look at the number after the line. 2 is less than 5, so the 3 does not
    change
    To keep it in the same order as 32 and a bit, add 0.
    Answer 30.
3. Correct 2864 to 2 significant figures.
    Put in the cut-off line – 28/64.
    Look at the number after the line. 6 is more than 5, so you must add 1
    to the 8.
    To keep it in the thousands add two 0's.
    Answer 2900
4. Correct to 2 SF 94.12
    94/.12
    Look 1 is less than 5. 4 stays.
    Answer 94
5. Correct to 2SF 0.01063
    0.010/63 (Remember 00's at the beginning are not significant, so the
    first significant figure is 1, and the second is 0 (a 0 *within* the number).
    Look 6 is more than 5, so 0 becomes 1
    Answer 0.011.
6. Correct to 3 SF 1,532,800.
    Look 2 is less than 5. 3 stays. Keep the same order of magnitude.
    Answer 1,530,000

Chapter 16
Percentages

The teacher probably needs to recap on some sub-skills first, if the students are coming fresh to it:

- recognizing fractions (see p 91).
- multiplying and dividing fractions (see p. 95).
- using decimals (see p. 99).
- multiplying and dividing by 10 and 100. They need to recognize the pattern involves making numbers one or more decimal places higher or lower.
- language used with regard to percentages. It is often heard on television in connection with buying cars ('0% finance') or with cheap holiday offers ('30% off if you book early'). Banking constantly involves percentages, so you might find some useful leaflets at a local bank.

  per cent. means 'out of a 100'.

  % means per cent. It means the same world-wide. 20% reads '20 per cent'.

  Words – per cent, more, less
  　　　 – interest
  　　　 – increase, decrease
  　　　 – profit, loss.
- accurate reading of calculator displays, especially with regard to money e.g. 1.06 = £1.6p   0.7= 70p   7.1= £7.10p

The percentage symbol

It sometimes makes this more meaningful to students to make three separate cards, like this:

and then rearrange them, like this

They can be put up on a wall as a reminder.

Using a 100 square to express percentages

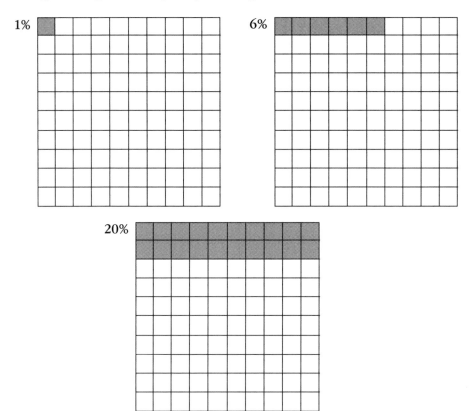

100 multilink cubes of varying colours can also be used to express percentages.

Common percentages

You can discuss some common percentages that your students are likely to know:

50% is the same as a half (1/2)   To find 50% divide by 2.
25% is the same as a quarter (1/4)   To find 25% divide by 4

Both 50% and 25% need to be compared to money – 50p and 25p. You can make cards with 50% and 25% on them and diagrams showing the percentages coloured in.

10% is the same as one tenth (1/10).   To find 10% divide by 10.
Spend some time on this:

* 1p is 10% of 10p
* 10p is 10% of £1
* Draw a 10cm line and find 10%
* Put 10 marbles in a bag and pull out 10%
* Fold paper and colour 10% of it

To find 10% divide by 10
To find 20 % divide by 10 and multiply by 2
To find 30% divide by 10 and multiply by 3
etc.

Use easy numbers for practice and bring in concrete materials. You can audio-tape some of these sessions and play them back. Once students feel confident about percentages they will be able to think of them abstractly.

Working out a percentage without a calculator – examples

Find 75% of £36.00   (75%=50%+25%)
    50% of £36.00 = £36 divided by 2   =   £18.00
    25% of £36.00 = £36.00 divided by 4   =   £ 9.00
    75% of £36.00 = £18.00 + £9.00   =   £27.00

Other examples to try:

1. 15% of £60.00   (15% = 10%+5%)
2. 25% of 4 metres   (for 25% divide by 4)
3. 20% of 200cm.   (for 20% divide by 10 and multiply by 2)
4. 60% of £24.00   (for 60% divide by 10 and multiply by 6)
5. 40% of 80kg.   (for 40% divide by 10 and multiply by 4)

Working out a percentage with a calculator

Find 6% of £5.00
6% means 6 divided by 100.   'of' means '×'.   £5.00 = 500 p
Press   6 ÷ 100 × 500
Answer: 30 (p)

Examples to try:

1. 24% of £114.00
2. 42% of 500kg
3. 81% of 620cm.
4. 11% of £5.00
5. 3% of 1.20m

Changing fractions into percentages

To make a fraction into a percentage we have first to turn it into a fraction
which is 'out of a 100'. Of course that is easy if it is 'out of a 100' already!

$$\frac{50}{100} \quad = \quad 50\%$$

$$\frac{25}{100} \quad = \quad 25\%$$

$$\frac{75}{100} \quad = \quad 75\%$$

$$\frac{60}{100} \quad = \quad 60\%$$

$$\frac{10}{100} \quad = \quad 10\%$$

If the fraction is not 'out of a 100' the best short cut is to multiply the
numerator by a 100 and then divide by the denominator:
e.g. to express 3/5 as a percentage, multiply 3 by 100 and divide by the 5
Answer: 60%

This perhaps needs some explanation, at least to the teacher!

What you want to do is to find out how many hundredths there are in three-fifths. This gives the sum:

$$\frac{3}{5} \div \frac{1}{100}$$

But to divide fractions we turn the second fraction upside down and multiply (a double reversal, see page 95), and this gives:

$$\frac{3}{5} \times \frac{100}{1}$$

Hence the need to multiply the numerator by 100.

It is a useful exercise to look at a list of school subjects with marks given out of different totals and discuss with the student which subject the person has done best in. The subjects can be put in order with the best first. The percentages can then be worked out exactly on the calculator and compared with the student order. It will be clear that putting them into percentages has great advantages.

English	13/20	(65%)
Maths	23/30	(77%)
Science	38/50	(76%)
Art	8/10	(80%)

Of course, it is easy sometimes merely to multiply the fraction by the number that is necessary to turn the denominator into 100.

e.g. To turn 32/50 into a percentage you just need to double the fraction (64%)

To turn 12/25 into a percentage you just need to multiply by 4 (48%)

But some students find this difficult.

Problems that deal with percentages:

The first step is for the student to understand the question fully in order to extract the fraction. It is valuable to spend some considerable time with the student working out which is the 'pertinent' number, which is to be the denominator. In a question about price reductions the 'pertinent' number is the original price.

1. In a bag containing 50kg of potatoes, 23kg have gone bad. What percentage of potatoes is bad?

   50 is the pertinent number

   $23/\mathbf{50} \times 100$ (46%)

2. Last Wednesday 5 children were absent from form 3. In form 3 there are 14 boys and 17 girls. What percentage of children was absent?

   Total children = 31

   31 is the pertinent number

   $5/\mathbf{31} \times 100$ (16%)

3. 32 trains left London for Scotland. If 6 were on time what percentage of trains was late?

   32 is pertinent (32-6)

   $26/\mathbf{32} \times 100$ (81%)

4. A shop is selling a coat for £42, which is a reduction of £18. What percentage is this?

   60 is pertinent (42+18)

   $18/\mathbf{60} \times 100$ (30%)

5. A motorbike is for sale at £322. When new it cost £846. What percentage reduction is this?

   846 is pertinent. Reduction is £846 – £322.

   $524/\mathbf{846} \times 100$ (62%)

Chapter 17
Probability

This has been divided into several parts, which can be taught in separate stages.

WHAT IS PROBABILITY?

Probability can be expressed in everyday language in various ways:

e.g. **in terms of opposites**
    likely/unlikely, certain/uncertain, possible/impossible

    with a halfway stage
    certain/uncertain/impossible

    or **more gradually still**
    certain/likely/unlikely/impossible

Students need to practise grading statements in this way to become familiar with the concept; they could grade sentences like the following,

    c for 'certain', **l** for 'likely' or **I** for 'impossible'.

1. Today is Monday; tomorrow will be Tuesday.
2. I shall win the lottery next week.
3. It will get dark tonight.
4. Today I am 168 cm. tall; next week I shall be 502 cm.
5. When I toss this die it will land on a 5.
    etc. Obviously you need an 'unlikely' grade for no.2!

Probability figures merely record in numerical form what tends to happen in practice over a long time, and this can be made clear by giving the students practical experiments.

EXPERIMENTS

1. Tossing a coin

A coin can be tossed many times and the results – how many times it comes down 'heads' and how many times it comes down 'tails' — recorded. The more times it is done the more chance there is that they will discover that there is an even chance of obtaining a 'head' or a 'tail'. Tallying is a good way of recording such experiments:

$$
\begin{array}{ll}
I & = 1 \\
II & = 2 \\
III & = 3 \\
IIII & = 4 \\
\text{JHT} & = 5
\end{array}
$$

They can be recorded like this:

SIDE	TALLY	TOTAL
Heads	JHT II	7
Tails	JHT JHT I	11

Students can take turns in tossing a coin 10 times, the other filling in the chart until they have done it 100 times. Results can be recorded like this:

Example

T	H	H	H	T	T	H	H	T	H		
T	H	H	T	T	T	H	H	T	H		
H	H	H	H	T	H	T	H	T	T		
T	H	H	T	H	T	T	H	H	H		
H	T	T	H	H	T	T	T	T	H		
T	H	T	T	T	T	H	H	T	T		
H	H	H	T	H	T	T	H	T	T		
T	T	T	T	T	H	T	T	H	T		
T	H	H	H	H	T	T	T	H	T		
H	T	H	T	H	T	T	H	T	H	Totals	
Heads	4	7	7	4	5	2	3	7	3	5	47/100	0.47
Tails	6	3	3	6	5	8	7	3	7	5	53/100	0.53

When the results are corrected to 1 decimal place, the answers are both the same – 0.5, showing in a simple practical way that there is an even chance of obtaining a head or tail when tossing a coin.

2. Throwing a die

A table needs to record the 6 possibilities, as a die has 6 sides.

Die numbers	Tally	Total
1	ЖИ I	6
2	II	2
3	ЖИ	4
4	ЖИ ЖИ	10
5	ЖИ III	8
6	ЖИ	5

The more often the die is thrown, the more likely it is that the numbers will even out. We say that there is one chance in 6 of any particular number being thrown.

RECORDING PROBABILITY IN FRACTIONS

Students must feel confident with fractions for this (see chapter on fractions).

To record 1 chance in 2, that is even chances (as in tossing a coin) we write:

$$\frac{1}{2}$$

and read it '1 out of 2'.

To record 1 chance in 6 (e.g. that of getting a particular number on a die), we write:

$$\frac{1}{6}$$

and read it '1 out of 6'.

The probability of getting an even number would be 3 out of 6, because there are 3 even numbers:

$$\frac{3}{6} \quad = \quad \frac{1}{2} \qquad \text{(when cancelled down)}$$

In recording probabilities you can never have an improper fraction, because the number of chances of getting a particular outcome is always less than the total number of possible outcomes.

The item whose probability is being recorded is put in brackets. For the cases mentioned above we would write respectively

e.g.
> P(3)
> P(even number)
> P(heads)   or
> P(tails)

Questions

(a) What is the probability of tossing a 'head' with a coin?
(b) What is the probability of throwing a 4 with a 6-sided die?
(c) What is the probability of throwing a number smaller than 4 with a 6-sided die?
(d) What is the probability of throwing a number greater than 3?

PLAYING CARDS

Students need to know certain facts about playing cards before they can estimate probabilities:

(1) There is a total of 52 cards in a pack.
(2) There are 4 suits – Diamonds, Clubs, Hearts and Spades – and 2 (Diamonds and Hearts) are red, 2 (Clubs and Spades) are black.
(3) Each suit has 13 cards. Jack, Queen and King are called 'Court Cards' or 'Face Cards' and have a value of 10. Ace has a value of 1 (or in some games has the highest value, 11). The others have face value 2,3,4,5,6,7,8,9,10.

Therefore, when dealing with the whole pack the number of possible outcomes is 52.

e.g. What is the probability of drawing an ace?

$$P(Ace) = \frac{4}{52} = \frac{2}{26} = \frac{1}{13} \qquad \text{(when cancelled down)}$$

Note

Cancelling down is always difficult for dyslexics. They can be shown how to do it on the calculator, as follows:

Press 4

Press the fraction key (which looks like this a $^b/_c$)We have referred to it as FK

Press 52

Press =

1 ⅃ 13 will be displayed, which translates as '1 out of 13'.

Questions

What is the probability, from a pack of cards,

(a) of drawing a Heart?
(b) of getting a court/face card?
(c) of drawing a seven of diamonds?
(d) of getting a red Ace?
(e) of drawing a card of value less than 4?

MARBLES, SPINNERS AND NUMBER CARDS

Marbles

A little bag is needed with an elasticated top or a drawstring. Different numbers of marbles of particular colours can be put in the bag to discuss the various probabilities:

e.g. 2 red and 3 blue marbles (total 5)

$$P(red) = \frac{2}{5} \quad P(blue) = \frac{3}{5}$$

or 3 yellow, 2 blue, 5 red marbles (total 10)

$$P(y) = \frac{3}{10} \quad P(b) = \frac{2}{10} = \frac{1}{5} \quad P(r) = \frac{5}{10} = \frac{1}{2}$$

To add variety, many different marbles can be used, or coloured beads or sweets if marbles are difficult to obtain, or you can use spinners.

Spinners can be either hexagonal or octagonal, and the sections distinguished by numbers or colours.

Questions

What is the probability of spinning an odd number?   P(odd number) =?
What is the probability of spinning a blue?   P(blue) is?

Number cards

If 20 cards are cut out, approximately 3cms. square, a different number written on each and put in the bag, they can be used for various questions, becoming progressively more difficult. (Care must be taken to ensure that the students understand the terms used. Table squares can be made, with prime numbers, square numbers, multiples or factors coloured in.)

Questions

What is the probability of pulling out:

(a) a number 3?
(b) a number greater than 6?
(c) an odd number?
(d) an even number?
(e) a prime number?
(f) a factor of 2?
(g) a multiple of 5?
(h) a square number?

Here 'a factor of 2' is a number that 2 can be divided by.
'A multiple of 5' is a number that can be divided by 5.

Chapter 18
Ratio and Proportion

A ratio is a relationship or balance between two (or more) numbers, and is written like this:

    1:6   or   3:5   or   7:4   etc.

It is always written with the smallest numbers possible (not 2:12 or 9:15 or 14:8, although these would give the same ratios). The ratio provides a small-scale model on the basis of which a larger one can be constructed with the same proportions.

Often the question is concerned with dividing a whole into parts, but these are *not equal parts*.

Here is a typical question of this kind.

'In a school of 400 pupils the ratio of boys to girls is 3:5. How many boys are there and how many girls?'

We then have the following information, with the small-scale model on the left and the larger school on the right:

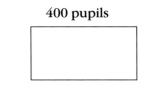

400 pupils

× ?

(8)

| 5g |
| 3b |

The total number of pupils for our small model would be 8 and that would be multiplied by 50 to get the number of pupils in the big school. Therefore we have to make the group of girls 50 times bigger to match, and the boys in the same way, like this:

Total of pupils in small model is	$5 + 3 = 8$
Number of pupils in big school is	$400 \div 8 = 50$ times bigger
Number of boys in big school is	$50 \times 3 = 150$
Number of girls in big school is	$50 \times 5 = 250$

Answer There are 150 boys and 250 girls.

So the method was:

FIRST add together the numbers in the ratio to determine the size of your small model group, then see by how many times the larger group is bigger than that and use that number to multiply the 'parts' – in this case the numbers of girls and boys.

The ratio may contain more than one number, but it can still be done in the same way:

e.g. 'A bag of money containing £100 is divided between three men in the ratio of 4:7:9. How much does each get?'

It is easy to demonstrate this sort of sum to your pupils by using piles of beans. There would be a large heap of beans consisting of 100 beans and a small heap consisting of $4+7+9 = 20$ beans. The large pile has 5 times as many beans as the small model pile, so each man's share must be multiplied by 5.

$$4 \times 5 \ (20) \qquad 7 \times 5 \ (35) \qquad \text{and} \ 9 \times 5 \ (45)$$

Answer: the three men get £20, £35 and £45 respectively.

Questions may be put another way round. The original question about a school might be put like this:

'The ratio of boys to girls in a school is 3:5. There are 150 boys. How many girls are there?'

The number of boys in the school is 50 times bigger than in the model (3). Therefore the number of girls will be 50 times bigger too (5×50).

Answer: there are 250 girls in the school.

They do not actually ask how big the school is in this question.

Once the general idea is clear the student should adjust to the question being put another way round in this way.

Another type of question is not concerned with a whole and parts, but with two numbers which change in balance with each other just like the items in the above questions, e.g. the number of objects that someone buys and the price that he pays. The changes have to keep the same proportion, just as in the ratio sums that we have been looking at. They may or may not mention the word 'ratio'.

e.g. '7 biros cost 70p. How much do 10 cost?'

This is obviously a simpler set-up than the previous sums, with only two figures to consider, and there is a simple way to solve it, called the **Unitary Method**, because it involves working it out for one item first.

7 biros cost   70p
1 biro costs $70 \div 7 = 10p$
10 biros cost $10p \times 10 = 100p = £1$

Or one can take a short cut and do this in one move, by using the fact that the dividing line in a fraction *means* 'divided by' – see page 58 and the 'Sums with Fractions' section – and write

10 biros cost $70 \times \dfrac{10}{7}$ pence

Your dyslexic pupil might find this complicated, but it is just a question of thinking which number to multiply by and which to divide by.

Here are two more sums of the same type:

'A recipe says that you need 280g of spaghetti for 4 people. How much would you need for 6?

$$\frac{280}{4} \quad \times \quad 6 \quad = \quad 420g$$

'Increase 12g in the ratio of 2:5'

This last question means that we start with 2 parts (12g) and increase it to 5 parts.

2 parts = 12g
1 part = 6g
5 parts = $6g \times 5 = 30g$
We have increased 12g to 30g.

OR

$$5 \text{ parts} = 12g \times \frac{5}{2}$$

'Decrease 250 ml in the ratio 5:3 '
This means that we start with 5 parts (250ml) and decrease it to 3 parts
1 part = 50ml
3 parts = 3 × 50=150ml
So we decrease 250ml to 150ml.

OR

$$3 \text{ parts} = 250 \text{ ml} \times \frac{3}{5}$$

There are some sums in which the numbers change in relation to each other in opposite directions, one going up as the other comes down, like the ends of a seesaw. This is called '**Inverse Proportion**', for example:

* the **greater the number of feet** that mountaineers reach in climbing Everest, **the lower the temperature.**
* the **more** men you have on a job the **less** time it will take.
* if a car goes at 70 miles an hour instead of 30 miles an hour it will take **less** time to cover a certain distance.

Consequently it is very important to decide first of all whether the answer will be *more* or *less*. The teacher will have to discuss different cases to help the pupil to make these decisions. It may well help if the pupil draws a picture.

Example: One man takes three days to dig a trench. How long would three men take? **(LESS)**

1 day's work for 1 man	1 day's work for 1 man	1 day's work for 1 man

Clearly if there were three men all three sections could be dug at once.
One man takes 3 days.
Three men take 3 ÷ 3 = 1 day.

Example: A car travels 10 miles at 30 mph, taking 20 minutes. How long will it take if it goes at 60 mph? **(LESS!)**

If it goes twice as fast it will take half the time.
At 30 mph it takes 20 minutes.
At 60 mph it will take 20 ÷ 2 = 10 minutes.

Examples for ratio

(a) Divide a piece of string 40cm long in the ratio 3:1
(b) Divide £80 in the ratio 6:4
(c) Share £56 in the ratio of 5:3
(d) Divide 72kg in the ratio 4:8
(e) Share 140cm in the ratio 7:3
(f) Divide 720m in the ratio 5:3:2
(g) Divide £150 in the ratio 7:5:3
(h) Tom, Pat and Jim won £180 000 in the lottery and shared it in the ratio
    of 4:3:2 respectively. How much did Pat receive?

Examples for proportion

(a) 7 books cost £70.00.
    How much will   (i) 2 books cost?   (ii) 9 books cost?
(b) 12 apples cost £1.80, how much will 20 cost?
(c) If 8 cans of coke cost £3.60, how much will 11 cans cost?
(d) If Sam bought 7 bars of chocolate for £3.15, how many bars could he
    buy for £5.40?

Examples for inverse proportion

(a) If it takes 3 hours to drive to the airport at 70mph, how long will it
    take if I drive at 30mph?
(b) 4 workers build a wall in 12 hours, how long will it take 8 workers?
(c) If it takes 6 men 8 hours to plaster a house, how long will it take 4
    men?
(d) Beth has enough food to feed her 15 birds for 10 days. 3 birds fly away
    so how long will the food last now?

Answers to questions on ratio

(a) 30cm   and   10cm
(b) £48   and   £32
(c) £35   and   £21
(d) 24kg   and   48kg
(e) 98cm   and   42cm
(f) 360m 216m   and   144m
(g) £70, £50   and   £30
(h) £60 000

Answers to questions on proportion

(a)   (i) £20.00   (ii) £90.00
(b)   £3.00
(c)   £4.95
(d)   12 bars

Answers to questions on inverse proportion

(a)   7 hours
(b)   6 hours
(c)   12 hours
(d) $12\frac{1}{2}$ days

Chapter 19
A useful procedure for tackling mathematics problems

The first thing to do with a question in maths which sets a problem is obviously to read it through very carefully to make sure that you have read it accurately. However, you then have to read it again from a mathematical point of view, which is different from reading a story. You have to think carefully what are the *important* facts from the point of the view of the sum, and ignore the unimportant things that you are told, the story element. Also look out for the first facts being put a different way round in the course of the question as in this example.

Example:

In two hours John cycled 18 miles. If he keeps going at the same speed, how far will he have got after $3^1/_2$ hours?

Here it is *unimportant* that the boy is called John, and that he did the journey on a bicycle – until you need to state the answer in a sentence at the end. Also note that the time is given before the distance at the beginning, but at the end of the question they mention distance first and time afterwards.

Try this way of tackling a problem:

1. Read the question carefully twice.
2. Underline or highlight the important facts in it, especially the figures. (If you are using a text book you may have to copy them on to a piece of paper instead. **Copy them carefully.**)
3. Put it into your own words; draw a diagram if that helps, so that you fully understand what the problem is about and what you are asked for.
4. Think what are the mathematical operations that you need to work it out, and write them down.

5. Estimate first – by rounding the numbers – the sort of answer you expect, and then do the sum.
6. Check the answer against the estimate.
7. Write out the answer as a full sentence.

Example:
In two hours John cycled 18 miles. If he keeps going at the same speed, how far will he have got after $3\frac{1}{2}$ hours?

1. Have you read it twice?
2. Underline 'two hours' '18 miles' 'how far' and '$3\frac{1}{2}$ hours'.
3. 'This chap went 18 miles in two hours; they want to know how far he got in $3\frac{1}{2}$ hours'

     2 hours   18 miles
     $3\frac{1}{2}$ hours   ?

4. I've got to *divide* $3\frac{1}{2}$ hours by 2, then *multiply* 18 by that number. (Or perhaps it will be easier if I first find out how far he went in 1 hour.)

     1 hour   18 miles divided by 2
     3 hours   3 times the answer
     1/2 hour   half the distance for 1 hour
     Add the last two together

5. Estimate the answer. $3\frac{1}{2}$ hours is more than 2 hours, but less than 4 hours (twice as long). As he does approximately 20 miles in 2 hours the answer will be more than 20 but less than 40.
Do the calculation set out in No.4 above

     1 hour   9 miles
     3 hours   27 miles
     $\frac{1}{2}$ hour $4\frac{1}{2}$ miles
     ―――――――
     $3\frac{1}{2}$ hours $31\frac{1}{2}$ miles

6. This answer is under 40, but more than 20, so it seems about right.
7. Answer: 'John would cycle $31\frac{1}{2}$ miles in $3\frac{1}{2}$ hours.'
Students might like to copy down these guidelines and keep them handy.

In the first 10 or 12 problems given for practice in Appendix A10, they may not need them, but for those e.g. from 16 onwards they will probably find them useful.

Appendix

A1 The National Numeracy Strategy

The National Numeracy Strategy which has now been implemented throughout England has many positive elements that can only benefit students with learning difficulties in mathematics.

Teachers should have high expectations of their students and will encourage them to develop coping procedures with all topics, which in turn will encourage discussion. The goals set will be limited but achievable, as ongoing assessment is mandatory. Clear objectives will be written down, which means that careful planning, well organized resources and suitably organized classes with the necessary support staff will be available for those students who find mathematics difficult.

Teaching will be multisensory at all stages, using number squares and number lines. A positive part of the strategy helps by using unit, tens and hundred number cards which are placed on each student's desk every lesson. This concrete apparatus is a visual aid which will greatly help dyslexic students to understand place value, which is always so difficult for them. This focus on place value will occur at every level, thereby reinforcing the concept.

If students put the following cards together they will read the number 631. It is an easy task for them to see that 631 is made up of 6 hundreds, 3 tens and 1 unit. This is called partitioning.

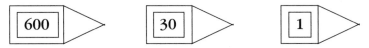

Estimation is encouraged throughout the scheme from year 1 so that the dyslexic student will gain in confidence from an early age by developing this most important skill.

The importance of understanding the language of maths has led to vocabulary lists for every topic to have a high priority, so while some long multi-syllabic words may cause difficulty for dyslexic students it will help if teachers are aware of their difficulties. Focus on number words (1, 10,

20...100, 200...1000, etc.) will help dyslexic students become familiar with the language that they will see around their classroom.

Every lesson begins with an oral session and ends with a plenary session. The oral session may enable dyslexic students to show their strengths if they are confident in the procedure. Counting aloud initially in 2s, 5s, 10s is reassuring as most dyslexic students that we have worked with are confident with these times tables. The many visual aids used with the scheme may help with the recognition of other numbers patterns. The plenary session which ends each lesson is a collation of work done in the lesson at all levels, focusing on the specific topic of the day encouraged and led by the teacher. This allows all students either to speak about what they have done or listen to others describe their findings. Any anxiety students may have in mathematics could be helped with the 'routine' of the mathematics lesson.

Mental calculations are now an important part of each lesson. Students with difficulties in mathematics are encouraged to take part in this session. Dyslexic students who have a slow processing ability may find these class lessons quite daunting but are to be helped by being encouraged to develop strategies to make helpful, meaningful personal 'jottings' and simple notes, which will enable them perhaps to reach the same correct answer as everyone else. While this may not be successful every time, there is a chance that with a good teacher keeping an eye on all students, plus a classroom assistant to step in with appropriate help, then maybe they will begin to 'see' how to participate in these sessions without too much mental anguish.

Dyslexic students often have problems with changing from horizontal presentation of calculations to vertical, many reversing numbers or simply misreading them, so not even being in a position to start correctly. Now that students are using number lines to see the value of each number in respect to other numbers on the number line, as well as being encouraged to 'add on' for both addition and subtraction, dyslexic students are greatly helped with these visual calculations. Also having to read numbers from left to right and moving along a number line from left to right avoids any change in directional thought.

Some examples of these problems
(a)   68 + 37

Horizontal	Vertical
68 + 37	$\begin{array}{r} 68 \\ +37 \\ \hline \end{array}$
Say numbers aloud e.g. sixty eight plus thirty seven	Say number in column with no relation to size e.g. eight plus seven and six plus three, not sixty plus thirty

Using Number Lines
(a) 68 + 37

* Start with the biggest number 68
* add on in 10s for the 30
* then 2 and 5

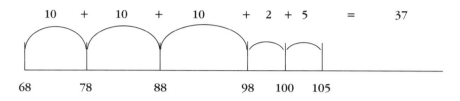

The answer is 68 + 37 = 105

(b)   6000 – 312
                    Horizontal presentation   Vertical presentation

                    6000 – 312   6000
                                                                        –   312

This is easier for some students by counting on a number line

Start with the 312
* add on 8 to make 320
* +80 to make 400
* +600 to reach 1000
* count in 1000s until 6000 is reached

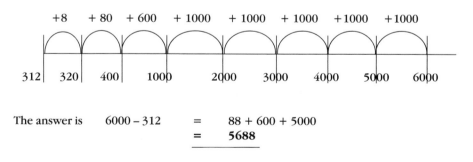

The answer is   6000 – 312   =   88 + 600 + 5000
                                               =   **5688**

The National Numeracy Strategy also encourages the use of Information Communication Technology (ICT), which can only be beneficial for dyslexic students as the majority of our students have all shown great expertise on the computer. This emphasis on technology will allow them to show their strengths, which in turn will promote self-esteem and confidence as well as assisting them with place value. Use of calculators also makes lessons exciting.

A2 100 Number Square and Number Grid

1	2	3	4	5	6	7	8	9	10
11	12	13	14	15	16	17	18	19	20
21	22	23	24	25	26	27	28	29	30
31	32	33	34	35	36	37	38	39	40
41	42	43	44	45	46	47	48	49	50
51	52	53	54	55	56	57	58	59	60
61	62	63	64	65	66	67	68	69	70
71	72	73	74	75	76	77	78	79	80
81	82	83	84	85	86	87	88	89	90
91	92	93	94	95	96	97	98	99	100

1	2	3	4	5	6	7	8	9	10	11	12
2	4	6	8	10	12	14	16	18	20	22	24
3	6	9	12	15	18	21	24	27	30	33	36
4	8	12	16	20	24	28	32	36	40	44	48
5	10	15	20	25	30	35	40	45	50	55	60
6	12	18	24	30	36	42	48	54	60	66	72
7	14	21	28	35	42	49	56	63	70	77	84
8	16	24	32	40	48	56	64	72	80	88	96
9	18	27	36	45	54	63	72	81	90	99	108
10	20	30	40	50	60	70	80	90	100	110	120
11	22	33	44	55	66	77	88	99	110	121	132
12	24	36	48	60	72	84	96	108	120	132	144
	2	3	4	5	6	7	8	9	10	11	12

A3 Times Table Exercises

Photocopy, laminate and cut up into individual cards then use felt tip pen to connect correct answers.

(1) Practice in 0s, 1s, 2s, & 3s

0×3	=	18	2×3	=	14	0×2	=	27	3×3	=	18
2×2	=	12	7×2	=	6	2×3	=	14	6×3	=	0
5×3	=	3	3×3	=	4	3×9	=	24	8×2	=	9
2×9	=	0	0×0	=	18	7×2	=	0	7×0	=	10
7×3	=	4	2×2	=	9	8×3	=	12	5×2	=	16
6×2	=	15	9×2	=	16	2×6	=	6	2×2	=	27
1×3	=	6	5×3	=	15	7×3	=	21	3×2	=	2
4×3	=	30	2×9	=	0	1×3	=	0	9×3	=	4
2×3	=	21	8×2	=	15	3×7	=	21	1×2	=	21
3×10	=	12	5×3	=	18	0×3	=	3	7×3	=	6

(2) Practice in 4s, 5s, 6s, & 7s

0×5	=	63	6×2	=	63	4×5	=	15	3×7	=	14
6×2	=	24	1×5	=	0	7×3	=	6	6×3	=	10
5×8	=	0	7×9	=	12	9×6	=	20	7×9	=	21
7×9	=	6	0×7	=	18	3×5	=	21	7×2	=	6
4×6	=	12	9×6	=	5	1×6	=	54	2×5	=	18
6×1	=	40	3×6	=	54	8×6	=	18	1×6	=	63
9×5	=	56	8×7	=	14	5×3	=	7	7×3	=	25
10×7	=	18	7×3	=	45	6×3	=	21	9×7	=	0
8×7	=	70	2×7	=	56	1×7	=	15	5×5	=	63
3×6	=	45	9×5	=	21	7×3	=	48	0×7	=	21

(3) Practice in 8s, 9s, & 10s

2×7	=	16	0×9	=	27	3×8	=	16	5×8	=	20
8×2	=	45	9×3	=	56	6×7	=	40	7×9	=	18
4×8	=	70	3×8	=	80	8×2	=	42	2×10	=	50
5×9	=	50	8×7	=	0	9×7	=	24	9×2	=	24
7×10	=	14	8×10	=	24	5×8	=	63	10×5	=	40
8×1	=	32	2×9	=	10	8×8	=	48	0×9	=	63
10×5	=	24	9×0	=	18	10×4	=	81	8×3	=	72
9×7	=	8	1×10	=	0	3×9	=	64	2×8	=	0
3×8	=	9	7×8	=	50	6×8	=	27	7×8	=	56
1×9	=	63	5×10	=	56	9×9	=	40	8×9	=	16

(4) Practice in all tables

0×9	=	35	3×7	=	56	3×8	=	30	10×7	=	10
6×3	=	49	6×7	=	10	6×9	=	16	8×3	=	70
5×7	=	0	9×9	=	21	9×7	=	24	9×7	=	49
7×7	=	18	7×8	=	6	8×2	=	63	7×7	=	24
4×6	=	30	2×5	=	42	2×2	=	54	2×5	=	63
6×5	=	27	1×6	=	81	5×6	=	63	8×6	=	40
9×5	=	24	7×2	=	25	7×9	=	40	7×3	=	48
10×3	=	56	9×7	=	0	10×7	=	0	9×8	=	36
8×7	=	30	5×5	=	63	8×5	=	4	8×5	=	72
3×9	=	45	0×4	=	14	0×7	=	70	6×6	=	21

A4 Table Practice Lists

These lists are not intended for initial teaching of table sums, but for revision and making the number facts secure in the pupil's memory after they have been taught by a variety of other means, as suggested earlier in this book. The teacher will have to decide at which point to use each set for this purpose. It is obviously an advantage for pupils to have these sums at their finger tips, and the lists are a way of managing this which uses only a little time at once. Once each list is put on a separate card they can be used for individual practice at home.

There are eight sets of lists – A B C D E F G H. These are graded so that the A set practises table sums up to 2 times, the B set practises sums up to 3 times and so on up to H which practises sums up to 9 times. Inside each set there are eight lists, each containing eight table sums at that particular level.

Note that each set practises **up to that point**, thus revising the past sets. Also the table sums are deliberately put either way round to instil the principle that if you know e.g. 5 × 6 you also know 6 × 5, (the Commutative Principle)

The first set can be used as soon as the pupil has been taught this principle, the effect of multiplying a number by 0, and the useful ability to double numbers up to 12. The next set may have to wait a while if the teacher wishes to give priority to 10, 5, 11 times tables, for instance.

These lists have been reproduced by kind permission of Mrs. P. Hills, who compiled them, via East Court School, Ramsgate, Kent, which trialled them. **They may be photocopied for classroom use only, but may not be reproduced for any outside purpose or marketed elsewhere.**

A SET

SET A1	SET A2	SET A3	SET A4
4×2	11×2	2×6	6×0
5×1	2×9	2×0	2×2
7×2	8×1	5×2	0×6
1×12	9×2	6×2	12×2
2×4	0×10	2×1	9×1
1×5	1×8	2×5	2×12
2×7	10×0	0×2	2×2
12×1	2×11	1×2	1×9

SET A5	SET A6	SET A7	SET A8
8×2	7×2	12×2	1×1
11×1	1×4	3×1	2×9
2×8	2×7	2×6	1×8
1×11	2×10	2×12	5×2
2×10	2×3	6×2	9×2
7×1	10×2	2×11	8×2
1×7	3×2	1×3	2×5
10×2	4×1	11×2	2×8

B SET

SET B1	SET B2	SET B3	SET B4
10×1	3×4	5×3	3×1
2×3	7×1	3×7	7×2
4×1	11×3	3×5	9×3
3×2	1×7	2×2	8×2
1×10	4×3	12×3	3×9
3×8	6×3	7×3	2×7
1×4	3×6	2×2	2×8
8×3	3×11	3×12	1×3

SET B5	SET B6	SET B7	SET B8
2×6	3×7	10×3	6×3
5×3	11×3	3×12	3×4
6×2	2×5	9×1	3×3
3×2	1×3	8×3	12×2
3×5	5×2	3×10	3×6
3×9	3×1	1×9	4×3
2×3	7×3	3×8	3×3
9×3	3×11	12×3	2×12

C SET

SET C1	SET C2	SET C3	SET C4
4×8	3×8	9×4	11×3
3×2	1×4	3×5	10×4
5×4	7×2	3×4	5×1
10×3	4×1	4×9	4×10
8×4	4×12	5×3	2×4
2×3	8×3	4×3	1×5
3×10	12×4	12×4	4×2
4×5	2×7	2×12	3×11

SET C5	SET C6	SET C7	SET C8
4×4	3×7	4×11	2×4
9×2	6×4	3×6	4×9
4×4	2×11	8×4	4×2
2×9	4×7	11×4	3×4
3×7	4×6	3×12	12×4
4×11	7×3	4×8	4×3
7×3	11×2	6×3	9×4
11×4	7×4	12×3	4×12

D SET

SET D1	SET D2	SET D3	SET D4
11×4	5×9	1×7	5×5
5×2	2×8	5×7	5×11
4×8	9×5	6×3	4×9
2×5	5×12	7×1	5×5
4×11	1×5	3×5	10×5
6×5	8×2	7×5	9×4
8×4	12×5	3×6	11×5
5×6	5×1	5×3	5×10

SET D5	SET D6	SET D7	SET D8
4×5	2×9	5×7	11×5
7×4	12×5	3×9	8×5
5×8	4×4	5×9	2×4
12×4	2×5	10×2	5×6
4×7	9×2	9×5	5×11
8×5	4×4	7×5	4×2
4×12	5×12	2×10	6×5
5×4	5×2	9×3	5×8

E SET

SET E1	SET E2	SET E3	SET E4
4×6	12×6	2×6	11×6
6×1	5×11	6×10	8×4
4×11	6×3	9×5	6×5
6×4	4×10	10×6	12×3
6×8	3×6	6×7	6×11
11×4	11×5	6×2	3×12
1×6	10×4	7×6	4×8
8×6	6×12	5×9	5×6

SET E 5	SET E6	SET E7	SET E8
2×10	6×12	5×6	10×6
6×6	5×2	11×6	6×6
2×3	6×8	8×3	5×7
9×6	6×7	4×9	9×6
3×2	12×6	6×5	6×8
6×9	2×5	6×11	7×5
10×2	8×6	3×8	6×9
6×5	7×6	9×4	6×10

F SET

SET F1	SET F2	SET F3	SET F4
10×7	7×9	4×3	12×7
7×8	2×8	4×7	7×8
5×3	11×7	9×6	7×12
7×10	8×2	3×4	10×2
8×7	9×7	7×4	8×7
2×7	12×2	7×6	5×7
3×5	7×11	6×9	2×10
7×2	2×12	6×7	7×5

SET F5	SET F6	SET F7	SET F8
4×12	1×7	9×5	2×7
3×7	4×6	7×9	4×7
3×11	7×7	8×3	11×7
6×7	7×10	6×7	3×2
12×4	7×1	5×9	7×2
7×3	6×4	7×6	2×3
11×3	7×7	3×8	7×11
7×6	10×7	9×7	7×4

G SET

SET G1	SET G2	SET G3	SET G4
8×3	1×8	8×8	8×8
8×6	9×5	9×5	12×8
7×4	10×8	10×8	6×7
3×8	8×4	8×4	7×5
12×2	5×9	5×9	8×12
4×7	8×10	5×10	6×6
6×8	4×8	4×8	9×8
2×12	8×1	7×8	9×7

SET G5	SET G6	SET G7	SET G8
5×2	5×12	3×8	10×8
9×8	9×7	12×8	7×6
7×3	8×4	3×10	8×8
8×9	6×8	8×12	11×6
11×8	12×5	11×6	11×8
3×7	4×8	10×3	6×7
8×11	7×9	8×3	8×10
2×5	8×6	6×11	8×12

H SET

SET H1	SET H2	SET H3	SET H4
9×9	9×10	12×9	9×10
4×1	12×3	8×12	4×9
6×9	8×9	9×12	2×9
8×7	10×9	5×11	4×11
8×9	9×11	12×8	9×4
7×8	3×12	4×9	10×9
6×9	11×9	11×5	11×4
9×5	9×8	9×4	9×2

SET H5	SET H6	SET H7	SET H8
6×8	2×9	9×11	1×9
9×5	10×8	2×7	9×12
6×11	6×9	8×9	6×5
7×9	9×3	10×7	9×3
11×6	8×10	7×8	4×9
8×6	9×6	9×8	7×8
9×7	9×2	9×5	9×9
5×9	3×9	7×9	8×9

A5 Coinage

A6 Clock faces

A7 Fraction Diagrams

A fraction with a **large** denominator is **smaller** than one with a small denominator.

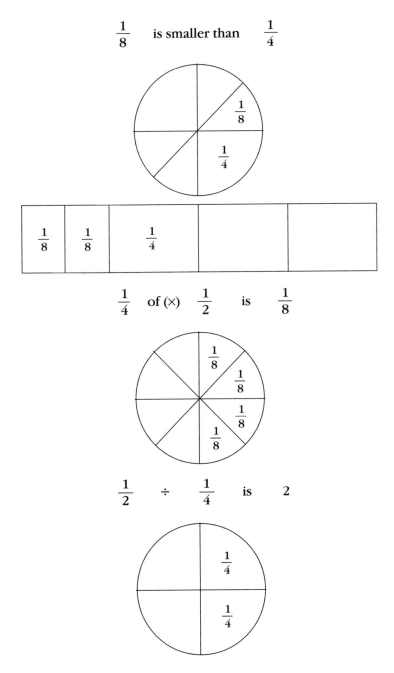

A8 Answers to practice examples within chapters

ADDITION (page 31)				
(a)	16	11	19	13
	26	21	29	23
	32	62	41	97
(b)	6	16	26	36
	10	20	30	60
	10	20	30	70
	9	29	69	99
(c)	17	28	38	48
	19	27	15	21
(d)	37	66	82	68
	39	59	87	77
(e)	93	81	75	82
	96	90	83	80
(f)	395	571	491	570
(g)	811	807	700	651

SUBTRACTION (page 40)				
(a)	8	6	4	2
	5	15	25	35
	12	35	46	70
(b)	9	8	7	6
	5	15	55	85
(c)	7	17	47	77
	2	12	32	82
(d)	13	23	41	22
(e)	17	44	69	29
(f)	37	54	36	69
(g)	135	421	212	342
(h)	325	429	8	749
(i)	173	490	155	585
(j)	169	589	214	682

MULTIPLICATION (page 47)				
(a)	4	8	20	10
	15	30	20	40
(b)	60	40	80	20
	60	40	80	20
	0	0	0	0
(c)	48	33	48	60
(d)	104	120	217	360
(e)	440	567	672	462
(f)	880	707	400	390
(g)	520	2530	3663	6960
(h)	120	220	620	920
	1200	2200	6200	9200
	820	630	3950	9670
(i)	2268	952	2035	8924
(j)	35,673	7733	52,287	18,900

DIVISION (page 61)				
(a)	5	2	2	10
	4	4	8	6
	7	7	8	9
(b)	23	21	31	11
(c)	41 r1	11 r3	11 r1	21 r2
(d)	25	14	12	39
(e)	15 r1	13 r3	19	15 r1
(f)	91	42	47	89
(g)	103	101	102r1	36
(h)	2	3	5	7
(i)	2 r16	2 r8	2 r10	5 r4
(j)	12	12	22 r2	53 r6

ADDITION OF FRACTIONS				SUBTRACTION OF FRACTIONS			
(c) 1	$1\frac{1}{2}$	$\frac{1}{2}$	$\frac{3}{4}$	(c) $\frac{1}{2}$	$\frac{1}{2}$	$\frac{1}{4}$	$\frac{1}{4}$
(d) $1\frac{1}{4}$	1	$1\frac{1}{2}$	$2\frac{1}{4}$	(d) $1\frac{1}{4}$	$2\frac{1}{4}$	$4\frac{3}{4}$	$5\frac{3}{4}$
(e) 6	6	$10\frac{1}{2}$					

MULTIPLICATION OF FRACTIONS				DIVISION OF FRACTIONS			
(a) $\frac{1}{4}$	$\frac{3}{16}$	$1\frac{1}{2}$	$\frac{5}{9}$	(a) 2	$1\frac{1}{2}$	$1\frac{1}{2}$	$\frac{4}{5}$
(b) $\frac{1}{3}$	$\frac{1}{6}$	$\frac{1}{12}$	$\frac{1}{8}$	(b) 2	$1\frac{1}{2}$	$1\frac{1}{2}$	$1\frac{2}{3}$

ADDITION WITH DECIMALS				SUBTRACTION WITH DECIMALS			
(a) 3.7	6.6	8.2	6.6	(a) 1.3	2.3	4.1	2.2
3.97	3.98	8.77	7.73	(b) 2.37	5.34	7.69	3.39
(b) 8.93	7.91	8.45	7.22	(c) 3.68	5.36	3.59	6.88
9.69	9.07	8.39	8.39	(d) 21.35	49.21	12.12	80.42
(c) 4.05	6.11	6.31	6.30	(e) 15.13	4.89	63.08	32.49
(d) 78.11	77.07	43.00	156.51	(f) 72.75	493.72	155.53	675.49

MULTIPLICATION WITH DECIMALS				DIVISION WITH DECIMALS			
(a) 4.8	3.3	4.8	6.0	(a) 15.6	22.6	71.25	692.5
(b) 10.04	8.10	21.77	36.09	(b) 15.5	6.1	2.2	
(c) 44.16	56.97	67.76	46.44				
(d) 88.36	71.26	100.30	41.34				
(e) 12.0	22.0	62.0	92.0				
(f) 120.0	220.0	620.0	920.0				
(g) 26.1	50.6	44.7	87.3				
(h) 1282	5363	73950	9675				

A9 More examples of problems

Examples of addition with money

(a)   £0.12   £0.50   £0.23   £0.47

£0.12	£0.50	£0.23	£0.47
+ £0.36	+ £0.46	+ £0.50	+ £0.22
£0.62	£0.95	£5.07	£5.33
+ £2.24	+ £1.01	+ £3.71	+ £1.40

(b)

£4.49	£6.32	£3.28	£1.04
+ £3.35	+ £1.59	+ £5.16	+ £5.18
£4.50	£5.46	£4.62	£2.81
+ £5.09	+ £1.81	+ £1.67	+ £5.57

(c)

£5.08	£2.85	£5.68	£2.87
+ £1.99	+ £3.35	+ £1.49	+ £8.34

(d)

£52.37	£57.96	£37.88	£71.85
+ £25.69	+ £10.84	+ £3.05	+ £63.76

Examples of subtraction with money

(a)

£2.50	£4.60	£5.80	£4.40
− £1.20	− £2.30	− £1.70	− £2.20

(b)

£5.63	£6.42	£9.75	£7.66
− £3.28	− £1.09	− £2.07	− £4.28

(c)

£6.61	£7.13	£5.30	£8.73
− £2.95	− £1.76	− £1.61	− £1.95

(d)

£22.58	£56.47	£14.28	£85.69
− £1.34	− £7.15	− £2.25	− £5.31

(e)

£20.81	£6.02	£93.92	£44.87
− £5.69	− £1.14	− £30.87	− £12.18

(h)

£427.40	£608.03	£525.72	£967.55
− £157.35	− £114.31	− £370.19	− £292.06

Examples of multiplication with money

(a)
$$\begin{array}{r} £0.24 \\ \times\ \ 2 \\ \hline \end{array} \qquad \begin{array}{r} £0.33 \\ \times\ \ 1 \\ \hline \end{array} \qquad \begin{array}{r} £0.12 \\ \times\ \ 4 \\ \hline \end{array} \qquad \begin{array}{r} £0.10 \\ \times\ \ 6 \\ \hline \end{array}$$

(b)
$$\begin{array}{r} £4.01 \\ \times\ \ 2 \\ \hline \end{array} \qquad \begin{array}{r} £3.50 \\ \times\ \ 3 \\ \hline \end{array} \qquad \begin{array}{r} £2.22 \\ \times\ \ 7 \\ \hline \end{array} \qquad \begin{array}{r} £6.01 \\ \times\ \ 9 \\ \hline \end{array}$$

(c)
$$\begin{array}{r} £5.47 \\ \times\ \ 8 \\ \hline \end{array} \qquad \begin{array}{r} £7.15 \\ \times\ \ 9 \\ \hline \end{array} \qquad \begin{array}{r} £8.78 \\ \times\ \ 7 \\ \hline \end{array} \qquad \begin{array}{r} £6.73 \\ \times\ \ 6 \\ \hline \end{array}$$

(d)
$$\begin{array}{r} £31.07 \\ \times\ \ 4 \\ \hline \end{array} \qquad \begin{array}{r} £20.15 \\ \times\ \ 7 \\ \hline \end{array} \qquad \begin{array}{r} £30.04 \\ \times\ \ 5 \\ \hline \end{array} \qquad \begin{array}{r} £12.76 \\ \times\ \ 3 \\ \hline \end{array}$$

(e) $£1.2 \times 10$ $£2.2 \times 10$ $£6.2 \times 10$ $£9.2 \times 10$

(f) $£1.2 \times 100$ $£2.2 \times 100$ $£6.2 \times 100$ $£9.2 \times 100$

(g)
$$\begin{array}{r} £5.32 \\ \times\ \ 10 \\ \hline \end{array} \qquad \begin{array}{r} £5.09 \\ \times\ \ 10 \\ \hline \end{array} \qquad \begin{array}{r} £4.51 \\ \times\ \ 10 \\ \hline \end{array} \qquad \begin{array}{r} £7.67 \\ \times\ \ 10 \\ \hline \end{array}$$

(h)
$$\begin{array}{r} £13.92 \\ \times\ \ 100 \\ \hline \end{array} \qquad \begin{array}{r} £74.66 \\ \times\ \ 100 \\ \hline \end{array} \qquad \begin{array}{r} £819.50 \\ \times\ \ 100 \\ \hline \end{array} \qquad \begin{array}{r} £79.75 \\ \times\ \ 100 \\ \hline \end{array}$$

Examples of division with money

(a) $8\,\overline{\smash{)}£124.8}$ $7\,\overline{\smash{)}£158.2}$ $6\,\overline{\smash{)}£427.5}$ $3\,\overline{\smash{)}£2077.5}$

(b) $16\,\overline{\smash{)}£516}$ $23\,\overline{\smash{)}£356.5}$ $37\,\overline{\smash{)}£225.7}$ $19\,\overline{\smash{)}£41.8}$

Money Problems:

1) Sam buys 3 books costing 56p, 22p and 13p. What is the total?
2) Tom buys 5 pens each costing £2.15. How much would that cost?
3) Sue has £10.00. Can she buy 2 bags which cost £5.34 and £4.89?
4) Lee has £50.00. He buys 4 spades which cost £6.20 each, 2 buckets costing £4.95 each. how much change will he get?
5) If Sam pays £7.97 for book and that is half his money. How much did he start with?
6) Jill has £50.00.
   She spends a quarter of her money on some tapes. How much does she pay for the tapes?
   She also spends half of the money left on a new bag. How much will she have left?

7) Chris has to pay 10% of the cost of a holiday. The holiday costs
    £240.00.
    How much must he pay?

8) Will goes to a café and has a beefburger costing £2.32 and coke £1.08.
    He then finds that there is a $1^1/_2$% service charge on his food.
    How much does he have to pay altogether?

9) If sweets cost £1.22 a packet, how many packets of sweets can be
    bought for £10.00?

10) The car park costs £1.00 an hour for the first 2 hours then £1.50 for
    each half hour after that. How much will I have to pay if I stay there for
    $4^1/_2$ hours?

Answers

Addition with money

(a)	£0.48	£0.96	£0.73	£0.69
	£2.86	£1.96	£8.78	£6.73
(b)	£7.84	£7.91	£8.44	£6.22
	£9.59	£7.27	£6.29	£8.38
(c)	£7.07	£6.20	£7.17	£11.21
(d)	£78.06	£68.80	£40.93	£135.61

Subtraction with money

(a)	£1.30	£2.30	£4.10	£2.20
(b)	£2.35	£5.33	£7.68	£3.38
(c)	£3.66	£5.37	£3.69	£6.78
(d)	£21.24	£49.32	£12.03	£80.38
(e)	£15.12	£4.88	£63.05	£32.69
(f)	£270.05	£493.72	£155.53	£675.49

Multiplication with money

(a)	£0.48	£0.33	£0.48	£0.60
(b)	£8.02	£10.50	£15.54	£54.09
(c)	£43.76	£64.35	£61.46	£40.38
(d)	£124.28	£141.05	£150.20	£38.28
(e)	£12.00	£22.00	£62.00	£92.00
(f)	£120.00	£220.00	£620.00	£920.00
(g)	£53.20	£50.90	£45.10	£76.70
(h)	£1,392.00	£7,466.00	£81,950.00	£7,975.00

Division with money

(a)	£15.60	£22.60	£71.25	£692.50
(b)	£32.25	£15.50	£6.10	£2.20

Answers to Money Problems

(1) £0.91
(2) £10.75
(3) No. The bags would cost £10.23
(4) £15.30
(5) £15.94
(6) £12.50, £18.75
(7) £24.00
(8) £3.43
(9) 8 packets of sweets
(10) £9.50

A10   More general practice

Use number lines, 1-100 squares, counters, etc. to work out these
    answers.

(1) What number comes before 9?
     What number is after 9?
     What number is 4 less than 9?
     Add five on to 9
     Count in 2s from 9
(2) Here are three cards

5	1	7

     What is the total of these numbers?
     What is the biggest number you can make with these three cards?
     What is the smallest number you can make with these three cards?
     What is the number if you take 10 away from the biggest number you
     have made?
(3) What is a half of 10?
     What is a half of 20?
     Split 50 into 2 equal pieces.
     If I doubled 50 what number would I get?
(4) Take 6 away from 15
     Subtract 9 from 35
     20 minus 12
     Double 6 and subtract 3
     Find a half of 18 and take 3 away

(5) **Make number cards 1 to 20**
   Put the cards that are multiples of 2 in a line
   Point to the cards that are in the 5 times table
   Put all the even numbers in a row. Look at the numbers you have left, can you give these numbers a name?
(6) Can you count in 5s to 100?
   Can you count in 10s to 100?
   Can you count in 4s up to 36?
   Can you count down from 20 in 2s to 0?
   Can you count down in 3s from 18 to zero?
(7) Write the following numbers in words

67	82	40
124	289	777
340	501	803

(8) Estimate a half of:

   30   52   98   140

   Estimate a quarter of:

   12   40   80   60

(9) Find pairs of numbers that add up to 60 and put a circle round them.

15	36	29	17	25
51	44	6	22	19
24	31	45	57	49
38	12	41	5	9
31	3	20	40	11

(10) What is twice 75?
   What is twice 101?
   What is twice 2.2?
(11) Sam has a card with a number on it.
   He says 'If I add 6 to my number the total will be 22'. What is Sam's number?
(12) Subtract 32 from 76
   Add 125 to 256
   Take 77 from 180
   Multiply 22 by 4
   Divide 86 by 2

(13) **Put numbers 1 to 20 in a bag**

What is the probability that I will pull out an even number?
What is the probability that I will pull out a number greater than 10?
What is the probability that I will pull out a number that is a multiple of 2?

(14) Write in the missing numbers

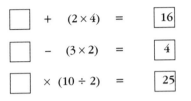

$$\square \quad + \quad (2 \times 4) \quad = \quad \boxed{16}$$

$$\square \quad - \quad (3 \times 2) \quad = \quad \boxed{4}$$

$$\square \quad \times \quad (10 \div 2) \quad = \quad \boxed{25}$$

(15) Divide 18 in the ratio 1:5
Share £16.00 in the ratio 3:5
Split up £36.00 in the ratio 1:2:3

(16) In a class of 30 the ratio of boys to girls is 4:6, how many girls are in the class?

(17) A box of sweets contains fruits and caramels in the ratio of 5:2, if there are 6 caramels, how many sweets are in the box?

(18) 5 books cost £40.00. Find the cost of:

1 book   6 books   10 books

(19) If 6 cans of coke cost £3.60, how much will 10 cans cost?

(20) If it takes 6 hours to make a journey travelling at 60 mph, how long will it take to make the same journey travelling at:

(a) 40 mph?   (b) 90mph?

(21) A painter working 6 hours a day takes 12 days to paint a house, how long would it take him to paint the house working at 8 hours a day?

(22) In a bag of potatoes 1/10 are bad.

(a) What percentage are bad?
(b) What percentage are good?
(c) What is the ratio of good potatoes to bad?

(23) Estimate the following:

(a) 1.9×3.1
(b) 3.98×2.14
(c) 42.3×4.01
(d) $58.1 \div 19.7$
(e) $\dfrac{103.5 \times 5.84}{99.7}$

(24) What is the approximate cost in £s of the following:
    (a) 5 shirts at £19.45 each?
    (b) 12 stamps at 26p each?
(25) Pam went shopping she bought 5kg of plums at 24p per kilogram, how much did she pay for the plums? How much change did she receive from a £10.00 note?

Answers to 'More general practice'

(1)	8	10	5	14	
(2)	13	751	157	741	
(3)	5	10	25 &25	100	
(4)	9	26	8	9	6
(5)	odd numbers				
(8)	15	25	50	70	
	3	10	20	15	
(9)	40 & 20	57 & 3	49 & 11	38 & 22	
	51 & 9	15 & 45	36 & 24	29 & 31	19 & 41
(10)	150	202	4.4		
(11)	16				
(12)	44	381	103	88	43
(13)	$\frac{1}{2}$	$\frac{1}{2}$	$\frac{1}{2}$		
(14)	8	10	5		
(15)	3:15	6:10	6:12:18		
(16)	18 girls				
(17)	21sweets				
(18)	£8.00	£48.00	£80.00		
(19)	£6.00				
(20)	9 hours	4 hours			
(21)	9 days				
(22)	10%	90%	1:9		
(23)	$2 \times 3 = 6$	$4 \times 2 = 8$	$40 \times 4 = 160$	$60 \div 20 = 3$	$\frac{100 \times 6}{100} = 6$

(24) $5 \times £20.00 = £100.00$ $12 \times 25p = £3.00$
(25) £1.20, $£10.00 - £1.20 = £8.80$

Word Problems

(1) Peter had a piece of wood that was 17cm long. He wanted to cut it into pieces 3cm long. How many pieces 3cm long could he make from his piece of wood and how much wood would be left over?
(2) If five cans of lemonade cost £2.25, how much will 12 cans cost?
(3) A car will travel 208km on 16 litres of petrol. How far will it travel on 30 litres

(4) If it takes 4 hours to make a journey travelling at 60mph, how long will it take to make the same journey travelling at 30 mph?

(5) Tom had a piece of wood that was 90cm long. He wanted to cut it into pieces 12cm long. How many pieces 12cm long could he make from his piece of wood and how much wood would be left over?

(6) A farmer has 6 men to help him collect his crop of strawberries. If they take 6 days to do the job, how many men would it take to do the job in 3 days?

(7) If 20 schoolchildren are going on a trip and each pays £4.50 to cover the cost of the coach hire. How much more will each one have to pay if 5 children are ill and cannot go?

(8) To buy food for a pet rabbit for a month will cost £36.00. How much will it cost for one week? How much will it cost for 6 weeks?

(9) If it costs £27.00 for 3 people to go to the cinema, how much will it cost for 7 people to go?

(10) The cost for 6 children to get into the safari park is £28.80. How much will it cost for 4 children?

Answers to Word Problems

(1) 5 pieces   2cm left over
(2) £5.40
(3) 390km
(4) 8 hours
(5) 7 pieces   6cm left over
(6) 12 men
(7) £1.50 each
(8) £9.00 for 1 week   £54.00 for 6 weeks
(9) £63.00
(10) £19.20

A11 Suggested materials and books

Sandpaper Numbers and Number Stencils	Consortium
Table-Top and Wall Number Lines	Taskmaster
Student Number Lines 0–25 (re-usable)	LDA
Decimetric Blocks (for place value)	Taskmaster
Unit, Long, Flat and Block Stamps	Taskmaster
Decimal Place Value Cards	Taskmaster
Tens 'n' Units 9a kit)	Crossbow
Slide Abacus (number bonds up to 10)	Consortium
Know Your Numbers Matching Game (up to 4 players)	Consortium
Addition Dominoes	Taskmaster
Subtraction Dominoes	Taskmaster
Multiplication Dominoes	Taskmaster
Addition and Subtraction Shapes	Taskmaster
Division Shapes	Taskmaster
Flip Flash Maths Addition and Subtraction	LDA
Flip Flash Maths Multiplication and Division	Taskmaster
Tables Disco CD (£4.99)	Sound Ideas
Number Books 1 and 2	Beam etc.
Calculator Darts	Taskmaster
Calculator Lotto (up to 4 players)	Taskmaster
Calculator Book (games and teaching tips)	Taskmaster
Coins	Mega Money Financial Sevices Authority
Money Dominoes	Taskmaster
All Change Game	Taskmaster
Linkapound (shapes adding up to a pound)	Taskmaster
Coin Stamps	Taskmaster
Teaching Clock	Taskmaster
Time Matching Puzzles	Taskmaster
Digital/Analogue Individual Clock	Taskmaster
Digital Dominoes	Consortium
Time (8202) and Measurement (8201) – books	Prime-Ed.
Fractions Basic Addition Dominoes	Taskmaster
Fractions Basic Subtraction Dominoes	Taskmaster
What Fraction Board Game	Taskmaster
Equivalence Dominoes	Taskmaster
Percentage Dominoes	Taskmaster
Percentage Discount Dominoes	Taskmaster
Percentage Fraction Shapes	

General

Henderson, Anne (1989) *Maths and Dyslexics*. Henderson: St David's College.
Henderson, Anne (1998) *Maths for the Dyslexic: a practical guide*. London: David Fulton.
Miles TR and Miles E (eds) (1992) Dyslexia and Mathematics. London: Whurr.
Chinn SJ and Ashcroft JR (1993) Mathematics for Dyslexics: A Teaching Handbook. London: Whurr.
Dyslexia and Mathematics: a Guide for Parents and Teachers from British Dyslexia Association, 98, London Road, Reading RG1 5AU

Useful computer software

Maths Explorer (K52) (Basic Skills) Granada Learning
Maths Explorer: Number (K51 and K52) (Basic Skills) Granada Learning
(They also have one on Shape and Space K52)
Maths Made Easy (ages 4–11) Prime-Ed Publishing
Sum One (early years 3–7) (Basic Skills) Resource
Patch the Puppy (ages 3–6) (Basic Skills) 4 mation
The Number Works (Basic Skills) Sherston Software
Amazing Maths (All Basic Skills) The Computer Centre
Maths Blaster (All Basic Skills) Ablac Learning Works
Micro-Smile (Essential Skills) Smile Mathematics
Number Shark (Games all areas): White Space Ltd.
Table Aliens (Tables) Sherston Software
What to Do When You Can't (Table Strategies) its
Learn the Times Tables
Multimedia Calculator (Flynn)
(can display calculations together with working with blocks and voice describing the working, also interactive multiplication tables to discover patterns). Obtainable from National Council for Educational Technology, Milburn Hill Road, Science Park, Coventry CV4 7JJ.
Supermarket (Shopping Skills) Resource
Crystal Rain Forest (Direction/Angles) Sherston Software
                              (Shopping/Sequencing)
Clockwise (Time) 4 mation
Maths Circus 1 and 2 (Problem Solving Skills) 4 mation

Addresses

*Ablac Learning Works Tel. 01626 332233
Consortium Tel. (enquiries) 01225-771320 (orders) 01225-771350
              Fax 01225-777920
              Internet www.theconsortium.co.uk

Consortium South West PO Box 1170 Trowbridge, Wilts. BA14 8XX	orders@theconsortium.co.uk
Consortium South East PO Box 135 Worcester Park KT4 8YY	southeast@theconsortium.co.uk
Consortium Cymru 4, Cathedral Road Cardiff CF11 9LJ	cymru@theconsortium.co.uk
Crossbow Educational, 41 Sawpit Lane, Brocton, Staffordshire ST17 0TF	Tel./Fax 01785 660902 Internet www.crossboweducation.com
*4mation	Tel. 01271 325353 Fax. 01271 322974
*Granada Learning	Tel. 0161 8272927 Fax. 0161 827966 e-mail info@granada-learning.com
*its	Tel.0178 8561991 Internet www.ideastakingshape.co.uk
LDA, Duke Street, Wisbech, Cambs. PE13 2AE	Tel.01945 463441 Fax 01945 587361 Internet www.instructionalfair.co.uk
Mega Money Financial Services Authority BEAM Education, London	Tel. 020 7684 3323 Fax. 020 7684 3334 e-mail info@beam.co.uk
Prime Ed Publishing (also*)	Tel.01203 322860 Fax. 01203 322661
*Resource	Tel. 01509 672222 Fax, 01509 672267 e-mail info@resourcekt.co.uk

*Sherston

Tel. 01666 840433
Fax. 01666 840048
e-mail sales@sherston.co.uk

*Smile Mathematics

Tel. 020 7598 4841
Fax. 020 7598 4838
e-mail smile@rmplc.co.uk

Sound Ideas,
117 Athelstan Road,
Bitterne, Southampton,
SO19 4DG

Tel. 02380 333405
Fax 02380 235128

Taskmaster Ltd.,
Morris Road,
Leicester LE2 6BR

Tel. 0116 270 4286
Fax. 0116 270 6992
e-mail taskmast@webleicester.co.uk

*The Computer Centre

Tel. 01487 741223

* indicates sources of computer software

Index